CHRISTABEL JESSICA
Artwork by CECILIA G.F.

DIVINE MASCULINE

HEALING ORACLE

DIVINE MASCULINE
HEALING ORACLE

Copyright © 2025 Christabel Jessica
Artwork Copyright © 2025 Cecilia G.F.

All rights reserved. Other than for personal use, no part of these cards or this book may be reproduced in any way, in whole or part, without the written consent of the copyright holder or publisher. This publication is intended for spiritual and emotional guidance only. The contents are not intended to replace financial advice or medical assistance or treatment. The views and opinions expressed by the author, both within and outside of this publication, do not necessarily reflect the views of the publisher.

Published by Blue Angel Publishing®
10 Trafford Court, Wheelers Hill
Victoria, Australia 3150

info@blueangelonline.com
www.blueangelonline.com

Edited by Peter Loupelis, Cherise Asmah and Marie DelBasio
Designed by Gemma Christensen

Blue Angel is a registered trademark of Blue Angel Gallery Pty Ltd.

ISBN: 978-1-922574-30-5

Designed in Australia. Printed in China with soy-based ink.

Contents

THE RECONNECTION OF THE DIVINE MASCULINE

The Purpose of This Oracle	12
How to Use the Cards	16
The Divine Masculine Card Spreads	20

CARD MEANINGS

Achilles	32
Adonis	35
Aizen Myoo	38
Anubis	41
Ares	44
Atlas	47
Buddha	50
Caishen	53
Cernunnos	56
Chaac	60
Dhakhan	63
Dionysus	66
Enki	70
Eros	74
Ganesha	77
Geb	80
Hercules	83
Hermes	86

Hiawatha	89
Horus	92
Itzamná	95
Jade Emperor	98
Janus	101
Krishna	104
Loki	107
Lugh	110
Maui	113
Melchizedek	116
Midas	119
Narcissus	122
Obatala	125
Ocasta	128
Òrúnmìlà	132
Osiris	135
Ra	138
Rūaumoko	141
Shiva	144
Śuddhodana	147
Thor	150
Thoth	154
Torngarsuk	157
Yarilo	160
Yeshua	163
Yum Kaax	166
About the Author	170
About the Artist	171

Dedicated to returning ease of emotion to the masculine, unlocking his loving heart and acknowledging and releasing his pain to allow him to freely feel and connect.

The Reconnection of the Divine Masculine

Once upon a time, in a magical land, a young knight took off his battle gear, wiping away the beads of sweat threatening to drip from his face. He glanced toward the honeyed glow of the sun, watching its shimmer fade as it slowly ascended below the horizon. As the peril of war encroached upon his lands, training days had become longer and more tiresome. If he hurried, he could still meet his love at the allotted time.

Creeping up behind her on the riverbank edge, the knight pulled his love into his arms. The maiden, who had been pensively connecting with her goddesses, squealed with delight and surprise. Talking late into the night, they shared their hopes for a quick battle and their aspirations for after the war.

Pledging themselves to one another for life, they believed that righteousness and love would prevail. They agreed to meet the next day at their special meeting place to bid each other an emotional farewell, not yet knowing the maiden would be the only one to sit by that riverbank again.

After the first week of battle, the knight realised his idealised notions of war did not translate to the brutality that now played out around him. During his training days, he had daydreamed about protecting his family, lover and the villagers of his home.

His convictions of protection, action and love were quickly beaten down to dust within him.

The heat of the blazing sun cracked the hard ground under his feet and bore down on his back as the young men he grew up with screamed in battle cries and agony around him. The battlefield was rife with movement and noise, and the overstimulation felt too much to bear. He shut his eyes, not wanting to see the ravaged souls and land surrounding him.

Swallowing his feelings so deeply within, the knight wondered if he would ever be able to feel again. As he watched the death around him and feared for his own at any moment, he hoped he never would.

One year into a seemingly never-ending war, he was still alive in his body but had a deep sense that his soul was broken. As his battalion passed through a town on their way to their next assignment, a group of priestesses invited the soldiers to their temple. Together, they found solace and comfort, seeking respite from the traumas of war.

In the young knight's mind, a different war was being fought — he had pledged himself to his maiden, and he had meant it. But now, was there any point? He probably wouldn't make it back, and even if he did, surely she had moved on. And if he did return, he would no longer know how to connect with her.

Everything seemed pointless. He made his way back to the temple one night, and there he felt the first flicker of something within him — connection, a stirring of the heart perhaps? It all felt too much, and within the week, he squashed it back down.

The war ended eventually. He survived. Returning to his village, he retired from battle with a body no longer willing to co-operate. His maiden, now a woman, had waited. He wanted to reach out but had forgotten how.

He turned more inward, living alone, feeling closed off and isolated in his little cottage. He avoided the crone who lived next door and the villagers who came for her medicine. He just wanted peace and the quiet of his cottage.

His ventures into the village remained short. He felt incensed seeing the young ones cry and whimper — emotion was not only uncomfortable, it now bothered him. Boys shouldn't cry! Don't they know men need to be strong? The once brave and confident knight now felt a profound emptiness, disenchantment and a crushing sense of isolation.

Yes, that magical land was Earth. Stories like this have run rampant, causing a disconnect within the Divine Masculine. It is time to break this cycle and provide deep healing to the pain caused by this disconnection from emotion.

For millennia, society has largely been built on a patriarchal structure — a system that places unilateral emphasis on the value of a man's power, voice, time and labour.

There is nothing inherently wrong with patriarchy; rather, it is how the foundations of it are built that matter. An integration of patriarchal and matriarchal qualities can provide a beautiful balance. The current structure has greatly affected all of society, including both the Divine Feminine (a tale told through the *Goddess Within Oracle*) and the Divine Masculine, a tale to be told today.

Living in an unbalanced patriarchal society has greatly affected the masculine. Counter-intuitively, a patriarchal society does not always work in the masculine's favour, even though it values a man's time and work more. Not only does the balance between masculine and feminine energy become misaligned—leading to a loss of connection and hostility between the two—but it also hinders his emotional safety. Living in patriarchy has led men to shut off from vulnerability, softness, ease of connection and a right to cry and feel emotion deeply and safely.

Men carry the burden of responsibility because of the value of their time, meaning we have seen them as the principal financial provider and responsible for keeping the family supported. This burden has weighed heavy atop their shoulders. This overexertion of the protective attribute of masculine energy was used extensively in war. The scarring from endless war and the disconnection from emotions are deeply embedded into the core of the collective, leaving the innate attributes of the Divine Masculine misused and warped. It is time to heal the fractured Divine Masculine energy. Earth is stepping out of the

Age of Pisces and into the Age of Aquarius and old, destructive paradigms are shedding, making way for a rebirth.

The purpose of this deck is to soothe the wounds that have been inflicted due to the nature of living in an unbalanced patriarchal society. As the resurgence of the Divine Feminine occurs, we have an opportunity to heal the wounded aspects of the Divine Masculine and build a new foundation based on unity and evenly distributed value — the integrated Divine Masculine with the empowered Divine Feminine side by side, hand in hand.

The destabilising of the patriarchy as it currently stands is a team effort intended to benefit and enrich the lives of all, making way for deeper connections with each other and within ourselves.

Welcome to the dawn of a new cycle and thank you for being a part of the expansion of consciousness.

The Purpose of This Oracle

These cards were created in honour of men in all phases — inner child, knight, father, grandfather and all aspects in between. This deck is for *anyone* who wants to explore and connect with their divine masculine energy — not just men but also those who identify as female or non-binary. Working with masculine energy is like a protective, enveloping hug — everyone deserves that feeling. Each person has masculine and feminine energies in varying degrees, so we can all benefit from receiving the healing available to us through working with both. Working with each energy polarity within you balances *yin* and *yang* and leads to becoming an integrated, whole being. And the place where masculine and feminine meet in the middle provides healing through balance and non-dual energy.

Take a walk through history, connecting with heroes, kings and gods of various pantheons, ages and energies. Some will call on you to feel deeply. Others will call on you to learn something new or to activate an aspect of your essence. Allow each card to take you on a journey deep within as they bring forward the teaching and healing frequency relevant to you. Over time, you will integrate these energies. Each embodiment of the Divine Masculine within this deck will surround you with love, support and guidance, ensuring you are not alone on the path of humanity.

INTEGRATING THE GOD AND GODDESS WITHIN

These cards are designed to be used with the *Goddess Within Oracle,* promoting the integration and balance of masculine and feminine energies, fostering harmonious relationships. When *yin* (feminine) and *yang* (masculine) polarities are intertwined, these complementary forces work together to bring you and your relationships balance and lifeforce energy.

Understanding the journey and plight of both the feminine and masculine can help soothe wounds caused by dualism and disconnection. Embracing the integration of both your feminine and masculine and relating with others will provide immeasurable healing, power, empathy and understanding.

Use the goddess and god within you as a way to clear energetic blockages and to unify your feminine and masculine parts. Suggested spreads are included for your own personal integration, and for seeking balance within relationship.

MYTHOLOGY

Mythology provides insight into how society has conducted itself in the past and how society views itself today. Mythology is not about whether the events took place but what the stories represent. Passed down through generations, they reveal societal values and perspectives. The language, themes and aspects of the stories that are frowned upon or celebrated can give you direct insight into how humans view themselves, then and now. This gives you access to limiting beliefs you may unknowingly hold so you may question them.

Your psyche may contain 'egregores'—group thought forms—that directly result from repetitive exposure to mythological stories. Perhaps there are things you judge yourself on based on inherited beliefs passed down that weasel their way in via your self-talk narrative. Questioning the narrative of how society was formed and the influencing events is a great way to dive into transformative work.

WORKING WITH THIS ORACLE

Refer to your cards when you want the protective support and guided lessons of the Divine Masculine. This deck is filled with healing energy for your inner masculine. Use it when you are experiencing heavy emotions or need clarity, and allow yourself to be embraced in a nourishing hug. The Divine Masculine is fierce, protective, action-based and underpins everything loving. When overwhelmed, he will be the rock you can lean against for respite and support; when you need to implement change, he will be the stern father guiding you toward action. He will give you the medicine you need—even when it is bitter—for he knows how to keep you accountable for your highest good.

Work with these cards when you need direction for deciding how to handle your current circumstances. Your fate is never set in stone. This deck does not predict the future but offers insight, clarity and encouragement to use your free will to determine your destiny. The Divine Masculine recognises your power to step into action to create the life you desire.

How to Use the Cards

The following instructions are suggestions to help you get started. There are no rules. Instead of feeling dictated to or restricted to working with your deck in a certain way, approach your cards however it feels good for you. Have fun, play, experiment and enjoy freedom within your oracle experience.

When first handling your oracle deck, take some time to develop a personal connection with your cards. You may like to create a sacred space where you can be present with the cards in ritual. A ritual can be as simple as walking barefoot in the grass or sitting in a favourite chair as you connect with your deck. For something more elaborate, add ceremonial elements, such as lighting a dedicated candle, burning essential oils or placing your favourite crystal near the deck. When your space is ready, energetically clear your deck (see *Clearing Your Cards* on the next page).

With your space and cards prepared, sit in quiet meditation with one hand underneath and one over the deck. Using your breath to centre yourself, focus your attention on how the deck feels. Invoke the Divine Masculine to infuse your cards with healing energy. Sit in meditation for as long as you feel comfortable.

Next, complete a card reading in honour of the deck itself. Ask for a card to represent the relationship you will share energetically, a second card to represent you and a third card to represent the deck. This will help facilitate deeper connections between yourself, the messages, the imagery and the Divine Masculine.

Another way to connect with your deck is to place it next to your pillow for seven nights as you sleep. Naturally, your relationship with your cards will continue to deepen as you work with them.

CLEARING YOUR CARDS

Regularly refresh your cards, so they are always at the highest vibration for accurate readings. Tap the deck three times as a quick and easy way to clear away residual energies before a reading.

Other ways of clearing your deck include smoke cleansing, sound bowl cleansing or placing the deck by a window in the light of the full moon. Between readings, you may like to set your deck in a bowl of salt or sit a crystal with a cleansing frequency on top of the deck. I like to use selenite, clear quartz or black tourmaline.

HOW TO DO A READING

Close your eyes and centre yourself. Anchor your energy to Mother Gaia by placing your feet flat on the floor and feeling your physical connection to the earth. Place one hand over your heart and the other over the cards. In your mind or out loud, call on your guides and your higher self to be present with you. You can use an invocation, such as:

My highest-level guides from the highest realms, please be with me and help me gain insight through these cards.

Bring your focus to the situation you are seeking guidance on. Hold your cards and formulate a question. The more detailed your question, the more focused the reading's intention becomes. Begin shuffling the cards in any way that feels comfortable to you. If you are new to pulling cards, be patient as you learn to intuit how long to shuffle and which cards to draw. There is no right or wrong. With practice, you will start to feel more sure of yourself.

Cards that fall from the deck as you shuffle are strong messages asking for your attention. Include them in your reading, and trust that they leapt out for a reason.

When you need clarity about a card in a layout, draw another card to give more information. This clarifier card builds upon the cards already chosen and deepens the message.

INTERPRETING THE MESSAGE

Each card is infused with an energetic transmission of the Divine Masculine. The card descriptions are written in a way that guides you to understand and adapt to the energies impacting you. Each card represents an aspect of being human and the healing path.

When you read the card messages, take note of the words that resonate with you. Take them on and expand your perspective for insight into your question. A card's meaning can vary each time it appears in a reading. You could pull the same card every day for a week and interpret it differently depending on what is surfacing for you on that day.

Understanding the meaning of your chosen cards may come instantly or after some reflection and contemplation. Look at the card's image and notice what comes to mind. The card name, symbolism, colours, body language or facial expressions may bring you a feeling or thought. Sit with the imagery of each card, allowing your mind time to process it. When you are ready, read the card meanings and feel the guidance as it pertains to your question. To gain inspiration on how to tackle your situation, read the story of the Divine Masculine that represents the card.

You do not need to come to one meaning. You are a multifaceted being — allow each part of you to have a voice. Your inner child will speak a different thought to you than your higher self, as will your intuition and logic.

The point is not to know which part of you expresses each thought or feeling. Instead, allow space for the vastness of all you are. Your subconscious and conscious minds will work together to bring you meaning from your guides, as will your intuition and logic. Take your time and write down any information that comes through to you. Some thoughts and feelings are fleeting, and sitting with them will be enough to allow for processing. Other themes will require more time to play out. You may like to explore your reading through journalling. Over time, reading your journal entries can give you deeper insight into how you feel about a situation and how you would like to move forward.

The Divine Masculine Card Spreads

SINGLE-CARD SPREAD

A one-card spread gets to the heart of a situation. Larger spreads have their time and place, but for a straightforward answer or when you don't feel the need to dive into the layers of your situation, go for a one-card spread. Use this spread to tune in to the overall energy of the query or to answer a specific question. You can use a one-card spread to represent the energy of the day, week or month.

TWO-CARD SPREAD

Two-card spreads are valuable in situations with a dualistic nature and provide clarity in simple decision-making. Be clear about the two sides you are weighing up. Assign one side Card One and the other Card Two. Shuffle the deck, select your cards and lay them down side by side. Interpret each card to give you insight into each option's benefits, challenges and lessons.

Some examples of dualistic meanings you can assign for a two-card spread include:

Do	Don't
Query	Solution
Yes	No
Past	Present
Mind	Heart
Logic	Emotions
Comfort	Lesson
Feel	Do

THREE-CARD SPREAD

More elaborate than the energies of a one or two-card spread, a three-card spread provides you with deeper insight into the layers of your query. Pulling three cards—to represent the past (Card One), present (Card Two) and future (Card Three)—provides a glimpse into where you've been, where you are now and where you are headed.

Another option for a three-card spread includes using Card One to represent the energy of a situation, Card Two to represent the most significant obstacle at hand and Card Three to determine how to overcome the obstacle.

I invite you to come up with your own way to use this spread.

COMPLEX SPREADS

Use a spread with four or more cards to conduct a deep soul search and to reach the core of multiple aspects of a situation.

THE LINGAM SPREAD

This spread offers insight to the energy of the situation at hand, the internal and external factors needing to be faced, and where the energy is headed.

Card One: The current energy of the situation
Card Two: Your internal energy that needs to be focused on
Card Three: External forces at play
Card Four: What energy to bring in
Card Five: The possible outcome after balancing has occurred

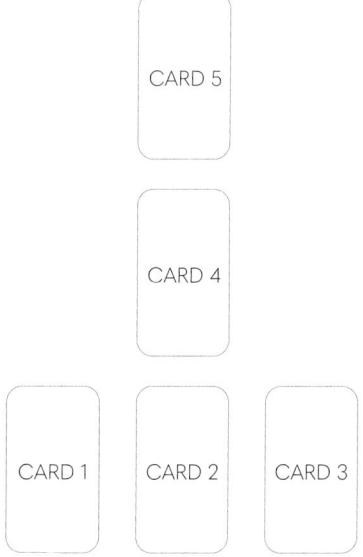

DIVINE MASCULINE ARCHETYPE HEALING SPREAD

You have within you many aspects of the Divine Masculine, each holding a unique energetic structure ready for you to draw upon. Connect deeper with the sacred energies of your inner masculine to know yourself more intimately.

> **Card One:** The Inner Child (the energy your inner child needs)
> **Card Two:** The Knight (the energy to put into action)
> **Card Three:** The Lover (the energy for heart opening and connecting)
> **Card Four:** The Sage (the energy to embody for deepening of wisdom)
> **Card Five:** The King (the energy to head towards)

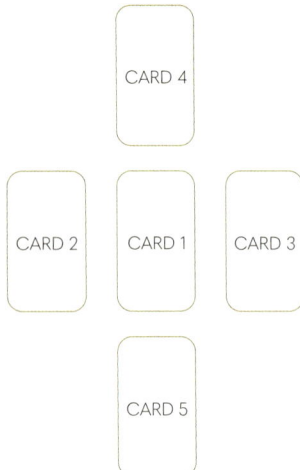

THE RECONNECTION SPREAD

Another option for a four-card spread is to pull a card to represent the best way to reconnect to your emotional, mental, physical and spiritual energy.

Card One: What card represents how to connect to my emotional energy?
Card Two: What card represents how to connect to my mental energy?
Card Three: What card represents how to connect to my physical energy?
Card Four: What card represents how to connect to my spiritual energy?

MASCULINE–FEMININE INTEGRATION

These card layouts are designed to use both *Divine Masculine Healing Oracle* and the *Goddess Within Oracle*. The purpose is to bring both divine masculine and feminine archetypes together to help you integrate both energies within yourself. This can lead to understanding the dynamics between yourself and others.

INTEGRATION WITHIN SPREAD

Integrating feminine and masculine begins within. This spread gives insight into the energy your feminine and masculine are currently in and what to focus on to strive towards balance and healing.

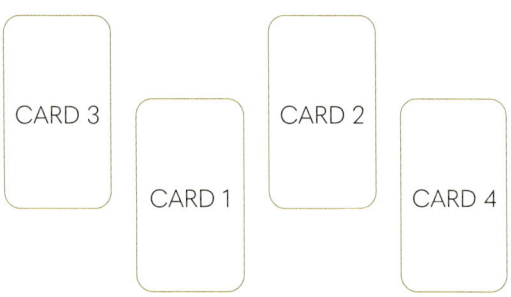

Card One: A goddess card to represent your current inner feminine energy

Card Two: A god card to represent your current inner masculine energy

Card Three: A goddess card to represent what energy to focus on to heal and balance your inner feminine energy

Card Four: A god card to represent what energy to focus on to heal and balance your inner masculine energy

RELATIONSHIP INTEGRATION SPREAD

Our relationships are mirrors illuminating our tender spots, gently guiding us towards inner and outer harmony. This spread provides insight into the energies you are each standing in separately, and the combined energy of the relationship itself.

As relationships come in many beautiful forms, use the combination of *Divine Masculine Oracle* and *Goddess Within Oracle* cards that resonate with you.

For same-sex, nonbinary or polyamorous and other types of relationships, use your intuition to guide you to the spread formation that feels right for you. You can use one deck (whichever you feel resonates) or both; you will know what works for your relationship. Perhaps one partner is represented by the 'gods' and the other by the 'goddesses'. Or mix both decks and see what emerges. Again, use your intuition about how the cards and the spread represent and serve you best.

The spread shown on the next page is one example of many possible uses.

Card One: Represents where you are now
Card Two: Represents where they are now
Card Three: Represents the energy you are mirroring to them
Card Four: Represents the energy they are mirroring to you
Card Five: Represents the energy dynamic of the relationship
Card Six: Represents the energy to focus on together for balancing and healing

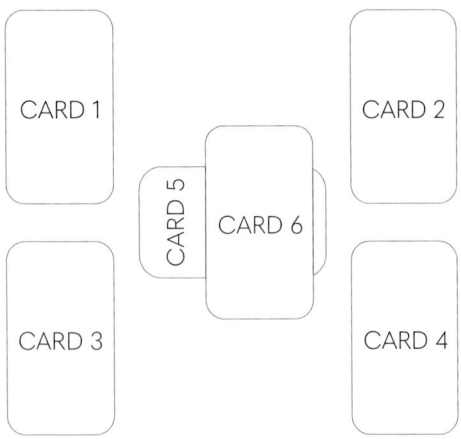

Card Meanings

ACHILLES

Examine your relationship with vulnerability. Cultivate environments in your life that provide time, space and safe, supportive relationships.

Perhaps the most esteemed warrior in Greek mythology, Achilles is accredited as a hero of the Trojan War. Born to mortal King Peleus and Thetis, a nymph and goddess of water, Achilles possessed immense courage and incredible strength. Out of a desire to protect her son, Thetis embarked on a journey to make Achilles immortal. Holding her newborn by the ankle, she dipped him into the Styx — the river of invulnerability separating Earth from the Underworld. Achilles became invincible apart from one weak spot where his mother had held his heel as she dunked him into the magical water. Discovering this weakness, a Trojan prince shot Achilles in his vulnerable place with a poisoned arrow, resulting in his untimely death.

ACHILLES' MESSAGE

Vulnerability is associated with weakness, yet exposing your tender parts takes immense strength and bravery. Social conditioning implies that it is not safe to be vulnerable or show softness. Many people have grown up hearing phrases such as 'boys don't cry', 'you're whipped' (when showing romantic affection), 'stop being a girl', and 'take a cement pill and harden up'.

It is no wonder men have not felt safe to be vulnerable. This deeply rooted paradigm has affected the entire population in one way or another. Not only has this squashed much within the masculine energy, but it has sometimes denied the feminine energy connection and openness with their counterparts.

It is time we break down these archaic societal conventions and work toward exhibiting our vulnerability to generate environments for others to do the same. This can be done by removing your masks and being as real as possible about your feelings, needs and thinking. It also happens by calling out how damaging it is when these antiquated sayings are verbalised.

Situations will naturally arise where you become aware of the patterns keeping you from being vulnerable.

Although vulnerability is a goal to strive toward, ease into it, one step at a time. After a lifetime of survival and protection mode, slowly opening to softness will help you transition into a new way of operating. Doing something before you are ready can result in you retreating and feeling even more traumatised. Awareness of the pattern and knowing you are not ready is still a monumental progression.

Choosing to prioritise your safety is an act of kindness to yourself when matched with making strides toward progress as the right opportunities present themselves.

ADONIS

You are enough; you are worthy; you are valid. Gaining confidence will help you turn inward to find the answers.

Adonis—the Greek god of beauty—was born as a result of an encounter between Myrrha and her father, King Theias. It all began when Myrrha tricked Theias into sleeping with her, siring a pregnancy. He was so infuriated by the trickery, the gods turned Myrrha into a myrrh tree to hide her. Born from this tree, the infant was saved by Aphrodite, who passed him over to Persephone to look after. When Aphrodite returned for him as an adult, Persephone refused to hand him over. Zeus, the god of the sky, intervened by allocating four months of the year to each goddess and four months of freedom for Adonis. Falling deeply in love with Aphrodite, Adonis spent four months by her side, ultimately becoming viewed as her counterpart. With a reputation amongst the other gods as holding astonishing beauty, Adonis is associated with rebirth, youth, attraction and fertility. Nowadays, handsome men are colloquially referred to as 'an Adonis'. He exemplifies the standard of beauty, not just of the gods of his time but also of the men of today.

ADONIS' MESSAGE

Assess your body image. Your worth does not come from your physicality. Your value is not born in the gym. Even Adonis probably found things he wanted to improve. Meeting the standard of beauty will not change the way you feel within without addressing internal belief systems tying worth to idealised beauty. Feeding into unrealistic physical expectations strips you away from joy. You don't need to be perfect to attract the right people. Those giving you the time of day solely because you possess certain physical attributes are not the people for you.

You were born enough and you are still enough. Everyone can benefit from developing their inner and outer qualities; however, it doesn't have to come from a place of not feeling good enough. Is your self-development coming from an intention of making yourself lovable, or is it an improvement to feel the quality of life available at your healthiest state? Be honest about where your desire to improve your body comes from — is it from a wellness perspective or a lack of self-acceptance? Your intention matters.

Comparison takes away from your unique qualities. Confidence comes when you develop an internal locus of control rather than an external one. Looking to external sources for validation, approval and direction is not conducive to confidence.

Give your inner being permission to start a journey of self-love and radical self-acceptance. It is not selfish to love yourself. When you adequately accept, care for and love yourself, you are less likely to forcefully take from others. Receiving from others is necessary and wonderful, yet tending to your inner world with nurturing care makes it easier to balance giving and receiving in relationships.

Healing is not about becoming the most lovable person in the world — it's about accepting and loving the worst parts of you, too. When our dark, twisty parts are seen and acknowledged for what they are, they can be brought to light. Look to your insecurities to see where to apply the salve of self-love.

Turn inward to find your answers. Embrace who you are — you no longer need validation to feel worthy of a place with your peers.

AIZEN MYOO

Become a master at expressing your anger via healthy outlets. Repressing anger can lead to reactive behaviour. Practise responding rather than reacting.

Aizen Myoo has been a deity within the Japanese pantheon since the thirteenth century. In Japanese Buddhist mythology, he is known as one of the Wisdom Kings, a deity characterised by wrath and protection. As the Wisdom King of passion, Aizen Myoo embodies rage. Often depicted with wild hair sticking up every which way, fiery red skin and a collection of weapons at hand, he is a fearsome sight to behold. He is an example of the inhibition of a person's true nature — the psyche imbued with anger. He is a symbol of the Buddhist belief that violent and lustful energies can be transformed into enlightenment. Besides his correlation with rage, he is also acknowledged as an exceptionally compassionate god who helps people overcome difficulties along their journey.

AIZEN MYOO'S MESSAGE

The stigma surrounding anger has led to repression and an attempt to turn away from and deny the emotion at all costs. Anger itself is not dangerous; the danger is in the actions unleashed by someone who does not hold a healthy relationship with their anger. Anger itself is a valuable guidance system that is a fundamental part of the human build. Pretending it does not exist within you can lead to it having a hold over you and becoming a volcanic-like eruption.

Anger is a primary emotion, directing you to an area that requires attention, protection or validation. It can also present as a secondary emotion masking grief, sadness, disappointment, shame or embarrassment. Feeling fury can seem less vulnerable, especially for masculine energy, which has been shunned from crying.

Other emotions can be too painful or seem unsafe in a society that dismisses softness. Sometimes, when someone is embarrassed, sad or disappointed, they don't even realise it. This is when anger flares up as a secondary response. The longer this continues, the risk of habitual anger developing occurs.

When repressed emotion lies under the surface, any minor inconvenience can become the straw that breaks the camel's back. Habitual anger is akin to a pot constantly boiling over — it needs to be emptied to cease the cycle. Shadow work and developing emotional intelligence, skill and regulation can assist in uncovering the mask of anger.

Changing your perspective surrounding the things that make you angry will help in the long run. However, any anger that already exists must now be acknowledged and felt. Anger cannot be let go of. It is released through movement. First, work on shifting your perspective around anger. Admit the emotion is there and permit yourself to feel it. Come up with a list of go-to methods that work for you, such as going to a rage room, running and allowing your stomping feet to process the fiery inferno within, or beating your pillow onto your bed. There is no way out but through, and you deserve the calm state the releasing of pent-up emotion brings.

ANUBIS

Strive toward a return to balance, but enjoy your time in the extremes. Contrast provides you with a profound enhancement of the experience.

The jackal-headed god of the dead, Anubis, is an ancient Egyptian deity associated with protection, mummification and the afterlife. His name in the original Egyptian language was Inpu, which inferred 'decay'. He is well known for his role in the judgement of souls in the Hall of Truth. During the judgement of the dead, Anubis would place the heart of the recently deceased on the scale of justice, balancing it against the feather of Ma'at, the goddess of truth. If the heart was lighter than the feather, the deceased would be deemed worthy of entering the afterlife. If heavier, their soul would be devoured by the demon goddess, Ammut.

ANUBIS' MESSAGE

Imagine the exquisite feeling of eating a burger after a week of only eating jelly because you had your wisdom teeth out; the pure bliss of sleeping in your own bed after a wild weekend of camping in the bush; the ecstasy of a hot shower after a cold walk caught out in the rain. Contrast is where life exists. Contrast deepens, stretches and builds. Being out of balance is necessary and good for us. Returning to homeostasis is integral for the health of your system; nevertheless, times out of balance are integral for living. So much living occurs through periods in the extremes. The most memorable moments in life tend to happen when the pendulum has swung from one side to the other.

The light and shadow, the masculine and feminine, action and rest all live outside the restraints of balance. Peaceful bliss is found in the centre; although drawn out for too long, it turns from peace to stagnation. You will naturally be attuned to when your nervous system requires you to err toward equilibrium.

Learn to stay in the present moment and tune in with your body, emotions and needs. This will help you become a pro at knowing when and how to bring yourself back to harmony.

Working on self-worth will give you the desire to look after yourself, knowing you deserve to have your needs met. Balance can often be found through the energy opposite to that you have mostly been in. If you feel out of whack, look to the other side. If you've been doing lots of shadow work, seek some levity. If you've been resting a lot and feel a state of atrophy, return to action.

If you were completely balanced in each moment, you would be bored with no growth, transformation or experiences. Contract and expand rather than just seek equilibrium. Similar to a rubber band shooting forward after being flung backward, you can experience benefits from times of contraction.

Swing forth on the pendulum of life, enjoying the highs, the lows, the ebbs and the flows, and recognise the areas that would benefit from finding some peace.

ARES

A hardened heart has served a purpose in protecting you. It is time to relinquish the hold of darkness and step back into flow.

One of the twelve Olympians—the major ancient Hellenic gods—Ares is the god of war, also known as the spirit of battle. Although his parents, Zeus and Hera, were two of the most renowned Olympians, Ares was not considered as well-loved or respected. Connotations with brutality, lack of morality and the trauma of war affected his reputation. He would arrive to battle in a chariot drawn by four immortal horses, accompanied by vultures and his favourite pet hunting hounds. Where Ares' sister, Athena, was associated with the wisdom and mental strategy of battle, he represented the aspects of bloodlust and unbridled violence. Ares began a long-spanning love affair with Aphrodite while she was married to Hephaestus. Together with Aphrodite, Ares fathered four children.

ARES' MESSAGE

Long ago, a part of the Divine Masculine's heart went to war and has yet to return. Traumas and behaviour patterns that develop collectively can claw in so severely that they become the new norm for generations to come. Our inner masculine has become exceedingly adept at hardening the heart due to the archetype of the soldier and the stigma surrounding crying and exhibiting softer emotions. This energy presents as a battle wound with a layer of calcification over the top. It is a façade, a tough exterior protecting a wounded interior. It can feel like the braver choice to be stoic, but it inevitably leads to hollowness, numbness and pain.

Being cloaked in armour feels safe and protective. However, when worn after the war has ended, the armour becomes the problem. The weight of that armour turns from the object of your protection to the very thing weighing you down. Protecting your peace is essential, yet so is living. Allowing the piercing of the shield around your heart takes immense bravery.

If you are romantically interested in someone with a seemingly impenetrable ice boulder barricading their heart, it is not your job to thaw it out. If someone is not actively seeking help and working on their issues autonomously, be cautious about stepping into co-dependency. Ensure you do not get sucked into a dark void of taking emotional responsibility for someone else.

Research the four attachment styles—secure, avoidant, anxious and disorganised—to better understand yourself and others. Avoidant and anxiously attached people tend to attract each other, becoming entangled in dopamine-hit-inducing, addictive to-and-fro situations. Working on the root causes and subsequent behaviour patterns linked to your attachment style will help you develop a secure attachment and an open yet discerning heart.

Sometimes, the only way to survive hardship is to harden the heart for protection. Nonetheless, once the hardship is over, it no longer serves to be in protection mode. Seek assistance from mentors to help you melt the ice keeping you from being vulnerable. You deserve to experience life from an open-hearted vantage point.

ATLAS

You are acknowledged for the sheer burden you have had to bear. The brunt atop your shoulders has been earth-shattering. It is time to shed some of that crippling weight.

Considered to be the most famous of all Titans—the Greek deities that came before the Olympians—Atlas led the Titan rebellion against Zeus. His father was the Titan lord Iapetus, and his mother was an oceanid named Asia. The first king of Mauretania, Atlas is associated with philosophy, astronomy and mathematics. The war between the Olympians and Titans—the

Titanomachy—was waged for ten years. As the Titans' leader, Atlas was the most severely punished when Zeus ascended the divine throne. Condemned to hold up the sky upon his shoulders, Atlas would endure this burden and carry the weight of the world for eternity.

ATLAS' MESSAGE

Responsibilities are a crucial element of life. Instead of drifting listlessly, obligations can give you meaning, structure, confidence and a sense of pride. Yet, that energy can shift to a burden when you feel trapped and boxed in by your commitments — feeling weighed down by the things you must do instead of viewing them as things you get to do. Everybody needs respite from their responsibilities sometimes, and for you, it's time to find some relief.

Certain responsibilities remain ever-present, whether they be from keeping up with the needs of being human, making money or from lifelong commitments such as parenthood. Then, there are self-imposed obligations that can be shirked. They may require letting go of societal expectations that you no longer want to follow or from things that used to be important to you but no longer are.

Participate in things that make you happy for as long as they make you happy. Continuing to engage in relationships, work and goals that no longer bring happiness is like clinging to decay.

Detach from what no longer serves you for the benefit of all involved.

Sift through the structure of your daily routines and the bigger picture of your life as it stands now. In what areas can you reduce your workload, and in what areas can you ask for help? Practise accepting help when people offer it, and practise asking for assistance. Loved ones often don't know we need support until we ask. Giving can be an uplifting experience — it's okay to receive. Start with finding a regular, safe place to share what is on your mind. A problem shared is a problem halved, both in the emotional release sense and in having a soundboard to assist in coming up with solutions and plans to implement change.

Create pockets of reprieve from the concerns of your daily life. Assess where you are overcommitting and why. Reframe your beliefs surrounding people-pleasing, stress addiction and the correlation between worth and productivity. Find respite through spiritual practice, hobbies and nourishing rest to give you the energy necessary to conquer.

BUDDHA

Accepting what has been does not condone the happenings of the past but allows for moving on. Release rigid mindsets and move forward into a future set on your terms.

Gautama Siddartha—the Buddha—was a Nepalese prince who became the Enlightened One. Born in 563 BCE to parents Queen Maya and King Śuddhodana, Gautama became the founding master and teacher of Buddhism. His mother had a prophetic dream that she would become pregnant with a son who would be either a king or a religious leader. When she passed away seven days after birthing Gautama, King Śuddhodana attempted to keep him from turning to religion. He surrounded Gautama with all pleasures within the walls of the palace, sheltered from human suffering. Upon leaving the palace for the first time at age 29, Gautama was so distraught after seeing the villagers suffering he went on a quest, renounced pleasure and fasted for 49 days. Seeking refuge from the knowledge that human suffering existed, it took time for him to arrive at a state of acceptance regarding the realities of the world. Gautama eventually found enlightenment by meditating under a fig tree, now named 'the Bodhi Tree'.

BUDDHA'S MESSAGE

If a friend experienced a heart-wrenching tragedy, you probably wouldn't tell them, "Ah, it is what it is; accept it and let go." That would pile on invalidation atop the agony and suffering consuming them.

Offer yourself the same consideration. Acceptance occurs several steps into a healing voyage; it comes at the hand of processing. Premature acceptance can hinder vital processes that need to happen before reaching this stage.

Toxic positivity and spiritual bypassing are both displays of premature acceptance. This keeps you disillusioned, opting for denial and repression of emotion rather than truly moving through hardship.

You don't have to 'get over it' to find acceptance. Validation of your experiences and emotions works wonders compared to trying to let go. Statements such as, "It is what it is," or "XYZ happened, but it's okay" do not move you toward acceptance — they keep you far from it. This mentality skirts around the issue, looking over it, under it or sideways. The admission of pain is what elevates you out of this mentality — "It happened, it sucked, it was painful, what now?" accepts that it occurred and allows for genuine moving on.

Accepting is not condoning; instead, it is putting a stop to fighting tooth and nail to change the unchangeable. It requires honesty about the fact that suffering has occurred. Not accepting means suffering indeterminably after the initial suffering. Something may be unchangeable; however, there are aspects you can change within your ability. That may be your perspective on the matter, how you move forward, or initiating paradigm shifts for future change. Take the learning, growth and motivations and bust through previously unopenable doors.

It is comfortable to stay in disillusionment, pretending that bad things don't exist. It is easier to pretend that things are different to how they are. Prolonging the inevitable will not help. Pretending your current situation is not as bad as it is extends your suffering. Accepting and experiencing the pain of reality now is tenfold better than continuing to deny the truth.

Accept what has happened to allow what will be to enter.

CAISHEN

Work on your 'lack mentality' to increase the flow of abundance. A feeling of security is awaiting you. Your relationship with money will be aligned with bountiful receptivity.

Caishen is a Chinese folk hero who later became revered as the Taoist god of prosperity and wealth. According to legend, Caishen descends from heaven to bring abundance to the people who worship him. It is tradition on the Lunar New Year to light incense and eat dumplings as an offering to him. On the second day, he ascends to heaven after providing blessings for the upcoming year. He wears a pink robe with coins around the hem to symbolise spring and feminine *yin* energy. He has a lotus motif on his chest, signifying fertility, and he holds a golden mushroom to symbolise longevity.

CAISHEN'S MESSAGE

Confront your fears concerning money to assist in stepping into a state of abundance. Check in with yourself and ask questions about why you have these concerns. Is it to do with the way you were brought up? What comments come to mind when thinking about money? These can be clues to 'why'.

As a collective, some beliefs need to be shifted, such as 'money being the root of all evil' and 'spiritual services should not be compensated for'. Change your perspective and see money simply as an exchange of time and energy, assisting in an infinite loop of giving and receiving. Money is neutral, and if it is in the hands of good, it can be used for positively changing the world.

Be grateful that your money has been exchanged for something good in your life. Each time you pay a bill, make it a small ritual. Be present and grounded when you make the payment, and take a moment of gratitude as you send off the amount. If you are paying your rent or mortgage, say, "I am grateful to have a safe place to live." If you are paying your electricity bill, say, "I am grateful to have this resource in my home so that I can live more comfortably." Over time, this will shift you from feeling that bills keep you from abundance to feeling like they are the abundance.

An avenue towards a prosperity mindset starts with knowing where you stand financially. Start a budget spreadsheet and be honest with the income and expenditures. Awareness is powerful. Once you see how the money flows, you will feel in control and know where to apply changes.

Executing a lifestyle within your means provides a sense of prosperity because you resonate with the vibration of 'I am enough'. If you have any debts, implement a plan—however long it may take—to reduce them. This shift will bring confidence and excitement for the future. The money put toward debt will snowball into savings and investments down the track.

If you have no debt yet still don't feel abundant, consider gifting to the community. Giving can be just as essential an abundance component as being in the energy of receptivity.

Make space to use money joyfully, enhancing the energy you associate with it. You deserve the money to have fun, too. Gain back control and feel your abundance mentality prosper inside out.

CERNUNNOS

Tap into your wild nature and relish in your freedom. Time in a relationship and time alone both have pros and cons. Ensure you maximise your time alone when you have it.

Referred to as the Horned One, Cernunnos is an ancient Gaelic and later Celtic deity worshipped for his kinship with nature and animals. With deer horns growing out of his head, he was part-man and part-stag, making him a mediator between man and nature. Known by many names, his origins can be traced back throughout the history of humanity within many cultures, and to this day, he is worshipped as a pagan god. A millennium old, Cernunnos—the Lord of Wild Things—ruled over the wilderness as a god of fertility, hunting, death and rebirth. Born on the darkest day of the year (the winter solstice), he has connections to the Underworld and wealth. The embodiment of ancient, untamed wisdom, Cernunnos is a great deity to connect with to learn how to integrate and embody the wild, chaotic aspects churning deep within you.

CERNUNNOS' MESSAGE

Rekindle your innate wildness and the sense of freedom that has dwindled within you. There is a delicate balance to strike between creating stability and freedom. It is easy to accidentally build a cage around yourself under the guise of establishing stability. A sense of security is important; physical elements are needed to stay safe. Nevertheless, freedom is essential for your soul. Time to roam free like a 'lord of wild things' provides deep soul nourishment and a reminder of the possibilities available when you spring out of your cage.

Times of wildness, sovereignty and fun lead to a well-rounded life. Whether you are single or otherwise, you are encouraged to look at how you cage yourself with your limiting beliefs. You have limitless potential; it is time to expand your consciousness so that even your wildest dreams feel within reach.

Although expansion is integral, there is a time and place for everything. Expansion is not the same as escaping.

Enjoy the phase you are currently in instead of constantly seeking what you don't have. This may be a time you look back on fondly, yet you feel like fleeing to the next chapter right now.

If you are struggling to find your independence and enjoyment in integrating your wild, free aspects, this is your reminder that there is beauty to be found in solitude. When you romanticise what you don't currently have, remind yourself that those on the other side glorify what you do have. When you are daydreaming about what you don't have, it is easy to glamourise it without considering the reality of it. Sometimes, those in relationships dream of the fun to be had single, while their single friends look at them, perceiving loved-up bliss. Enjoy what you have when you have it.

Time out of a relationship is just as impactful on your growth as time coupled up. In the past, marriage, property ownership, the nuclear family and gender roles contributed to maintaining rigid social structures. Now, the modern world is set up for the ability to construct different types of lives with less stigma and more accessibility.

Being single is a privilege and one that people from times past stuck in restricted situations would have dreamed about. Having the opportunity to choose a relationship solely for love and companionship is a blessing if it is something you choose to pursue. Being able to construct the life you want, when you want and however you want is a blessing.

Embrace the wildness of freedom, construct the life that brings out the most authentic version of you, not considering how it relates to another, but because it makes sense to you.

CHAAC

Take ownership of your mistakes. However, do not let guilt eat you alive. Learn from the choices you regret and allow them to make you a more understanding person.

Chaac is the Mayan god of rain and fertility, revered for bringing rain to Earth by striking the clouds in the sky with his axe. In Mayan culture, duality is reflected through the connection between destruction and renewal. Chaac and Ah Puch—the god of death—are said to work in tandem, with Chaac using his rain to create new seedlings, and Ah Puch nipping off the tips of the new buds. Another version of his mythology tells the tale of Chaac creating rain through his sorrow. Chaac had a love affair with his brother's wife, Kinich Ahau, the sun god. Upon seeing the pain he caused his brother, Chaac felt deep regret and sorrow burn inside for his mistake. As the pressure of the shame built up within him, clouds appeared in the sky. As remorseful tears fell from his eyes, the first raindrops fell from above as if the sky was crying with him.

CHAAC'S MESSAGE

The aftermath of a mistake can leave you stuck in a haze of self-ridicule and guilt. When you realise you have hurt someone, it can feel just as painful as being the one on the receiving end. It leaves you with an unpleasant feeling in the pit of your stomach and slowly eats away at you.

Guilt is an indicator of your goodness — use this as fuel for different choices made in the future. If you didn't care, you wouldn't feel remorse. Your mistakes don't define you, and your mistakes do not negate your goodness. How you move on from them can make all the difference in the world.

Reviewing past behaviours and seeing any toxicity you didn't see then is a marker of growth. Mistakes are fodder for learning and are experienced by all humans. You can't be living the earthly experience by avoiding messing up. Admitting that you have made a mistake is essential to help it not eat away at you, and it will ease your inner world and help mend the relationships with those involved. Trying to do everything in your power to avoid thinking about it will lead to mental anguish. Ensuring people feel heard and acknowledged can work wonders in patching up connections. An apology and humility can move mountains; accountability matters.

Counterintuitively, mistakes can make you a better person. Messing up moves you forward on your path toward becoming 'older and wiser'. Your character becomes enriched via your experiences — the good, yes; yet the bad deepens you even more. You become more understanding of others' flaws because you come face to face with your own. You want to do better because you know what being steeped in shame and guilt feels like.

If you have made a mistake, be remorseful, yet make sure you don't get to a place of debilitating self-hatred. There comes a point when you need to forgive yourself. Reflect, and choose differently next time you are in a similar situation. Move past ruminating on your mess-ups; you have more life to live.

DHAKHAN

Look to your family's history for clues to guide you toward areas needing healing. Break generational curses by changing patterns, ways of thinking and behaviours.

Australian First Nations mythology—known as the Dreaming—dates back 65,000 years. It centres around the belief that Earth was created by spirits who became embodied in the animals, people and various aspects of the land. In the Dreaming of the Gubbi Gubbi nation of South-East Queensland, Dhakhan is an ancestral spirit. Ancestor spirits emerged from the sky, the ocean and the earth in many forms to create all life, living still as facets of nature, representing the inter-relation of all things. As one of these spirits, Dhakan continues to live in deep waterholes and presents himself as a gigantic serpent with the tail of a big fish. When he travels from one waterhole to another, he emerges from the hole he dwells in and moves through the sky in the form of a rainbow before flowing into the next hole.

DHAKHAN'S MESSAGE

Collective healing is achieved through personal healing on a familial level. Ancestral lines pass down trauma, pain, patterns of behaviour and belief systems intergenerationally until they are consciously looked at by someone in the family. Creating a chink in the link stops pain from extending to the next generation.

Honouring your ancestors—all the beings who played a role in creating your life and family line—can resemble healing the ailments they did not get an opportunity to work through. It can also look like harnessing the gifts they have left for you. Retrieve the rich history, strength and resilience of those who forged the path that led to your existence. The aspects of those who came before you live within you now, connecting you through time and space.

Ancestral healing occurs by feeling the pain passed down without being addressed thus far. Look to your family's past and review the beliefs, behaviours and types of relationships that repeat themselves to see patterns you can actively break. Being a cycle breaker is not an easy task. You may be viewed as a disrespectful descendant by facing up to the family's shadow. The thing is, a revolutionary, awe-inspiring ancestor can also be packaged as a disrespectful descendant.

Step out of the shadows. It's no longer time to hide. You are not here to be a subservient descendant. A big part of ancestral healing is creating, and it is time to reframe the way you see yourself to a formidable ancestor. Stepping into that role with intention and purpose brings you into the mindset of a powerful leader and creator. Standing in the role of an ancestor who generates change requires feeling okay with rocking the boat, causing friction and, sometimes, being seen as the black sheep of the family. Holding a mirror up to the pain, patterns and beliefs that have previously gone unseen brings a sense of unease for those predisposed to turning a blind eye. Creating change is a labour of love you can offer to the generations coming after you.

Honour those who came before you by soaking in their wisdom and by changing what they couldn't. Provide for those to come after you, and produce new paradigms so they can lead a gentler path ahead.

DIONYSUS

Indulge your senses in pleasure and sensuality to connect to ecstasy. Look at the relationship you hold with sex and let go of outdated societal rhetoric holding you back from intimacy.

Recognised as the god of ecstasy, wine and vegetation within the Greco-Roman religion, Dionysus is known for having a plethora of lovers. Born to parents Zeus and Semele, the princess of Thebes, Dionysus had a dramatic start to life. He was saved by Zeus in the womb when Zeus' wife, Hera, devised a plan to abolish Semele and her unborn child out of jealousy.

Zeus sewed up the unborn Dionysus in his thigh for a time to keep him safe, making him twice-born. A patron of the arts and associated with pleasure and fertility, he represents the lifeblood of nature, particularly sap and juice. With a vivacious nature and a zest for life, Dionysus is a guide for those wanting to tap back into the sensuality of life.

DIONYSUS' MESSAGE

Just like a Venn diagram where two or more circles overlap, sexuality and sensuality exist separately sometimes and entwine together at others. You can have sex without sensuality, sensuality without sex and sensual sex.

Sexuality activates the body and sensuality animates your spirit. Combining the two offers an immersive, euphoric experience connecting the body to Source energy. Sex stripped of sensuality is often devoid of intimacy. Intimacy can be intimidating and requires profound, naked openness. This level of vulnerability can be a sensitive issue, not just in terms of the body.

When an open heart meets sexual liberation, a one-night fling can hold more love, connection and intimacy than a long-term relationship in some cases. Abundant aftercare, affection, openness and vulnerability can completely transform the act of sex to a healing experience.

Shame-filled narratives are one of the obstructions keeping modern-day daters away from deep intimacy. Talk such as being 'soft' for showing romantic love, being criticised for wanting to go home early to the 'ball and chain' on a night out and peer pressure to 'sow their seed' all serve to keep intimacy suppressed.

The rhetoric directed at women shames them for enjoying sex for their own pleasure and for indulging in multiple partners. Men are held in high regard for their sexual prowess and power, while women are shunned for it.

These two opposing narratives worm their way into collective beliefs, thus affecting behaviour, patterns and paradigms systematically. This shame polarity shows up like two magnets trying to connect but repelling and bouncing off each other. This opposing magnetic energy encapsulates much of the dynamics in modern dating.

Another obstructive dynamic in the dating scene is the prevailing preference for nonchalance, which is not only favoured but actively encouraged. Projecting an image of emotional restraint and aloofness is seen as holding the upper hand in this unspoken competition. There's a subtle contest to see who can maintain the most withdrawn, blasé or emotionally detached demeanour.

To avoid this, question your beliefs surrounding the feelings of embarrassment in showing romantic interest and consider working with a practitioner of your choice to identify issues of past rejection and abandonment that keep you fearful of intimacy.

Clear the past to find more ease in connecting with pleasure, play, sensuality and sexuality.

ENKI

Your ego is not the enemy. However, left unchecked and unseen, it can infiltrate your mind's reasoning and decision-making parts. Face your ego with love to gain insights and understanding about yourself.

From the region of southern Mesopotamia came the first recorded human civilisation, known as Sumer. In the Sumerian pantheon, the seven most important deities were called the 'gods who decree'. Enki (known as Ea to the later Babylonians) is the deity associated with water, knowledge and creation.

His name translates to 'Lord of the Earth', and he was the patron god of the city Eridu, where artefacts of his worship were found dating back to 5400 BCE. He was part of a trinity alongside his brother Enlil, the god of air, and their father, Anu, the sky god. Enki was in charge of and resided in Abzu, the ocean underneath the earth. One day, Enlil decided that humanity should be wiped out. Not agreeing with this decision, Enki delivered a message in a dream to a man named Atrahasis about an impending flood. Heeding the warning, Atrahasis built a boat and kept two of every animal on board to continue life on Earth. The great flood of Sumer lasted seven nights and was catastrophic, but thanks to Enki and Atrahasis, life went on.

ENKI'S MESSAGE

The concept of the ego tends to get a bad rap, yet each person has one, and it's okay that they do. Like Enki's warning to Atrahasis about the impending flood, your ego acts as a cautious signal, alerting you to potential challenges or disruptions in your life. It helps to keep you alive and thriving while you navigate life in a hectic world.

Denying the ego plunges your most human aspects into the hidden, murky depths of your psyche. The neglected elements transform into tendrils of darkness, coiling around your ankles, attempting to capsize and pull you beneath the surface. Seek integration and awareness rather than denial and repression. Pretending something does not exist does not make it so.

The ego is a tool for self-preservation, yet amplified, it becomes selfish, choosing self over connection, community and intimacy. It can go from the thing there to protect you to the very thing that brings you pain. A level of self-preservation is great to ensure your needs are met and you're not walked all over, yet too much of a good thing begets problems. An unchecked ego says, "Leave before you are left. Hurt before you are hurt. I am right; they are wrong." An ego left awry is threatened by being in the wrong. The over-inflated ego is represented by Enlil wanting to demolish the 'other' to serve the 'self'. It is capricious, devoid of kindness, understanding and co-creation. A healthy ego matched with consciousness and awareness allows for a beautiful meshing of self and others.

When awareness floods in, the ego pushed deep within can experience an ego death. The ego repressed does not die; it festers and flourishes; however, during integration, the parts that are no longer needed or no longer resonate come up to die. During this process, it can feel as if parts of you are dying off, and this can be extremely painful.

Integrating the ego requires raw truth, ownership and going deep beyond the surface with intention. The part within declaring, "I have no ego," is, ironically, the ego itself. Understanding allows for evolving out of habits based on fear and outdated programming. When you continually seek to understand why your ego or fear makes you want to hide, run, or act in ways that you feel are unbecoming, you can consciously change these behaviours through awareness. Respond instead of reacting.

Accept your ego as a friend, not a foe. Work on integrating its positive aspects while being aware of your shadow side. Once you do, this makes it easier to implement self-protective measures while also considering your connection with others.

EROS

You do not need to be fully healed to be in a relationship. Relationships can be integral to healing, providing connection and physical touch and meeting your needs.

According to Greek mythology, in the beginning, there was nothing — only chaos and the primordial void of the Universe. Then, the Universe fathered Eros, the personification of love. In an alternate retelling of his origin story, Eros is the son of Aphrodite and Ares. Eros—the god of love, desire and passion—would use his bow and quiver to shoot golden arrows into the hearts of potential lovers to incite feelings between them. Although he spent his days sparking love, he was determined not to have the same fate. However, one day, it was he who would be struck by love. Insanely jealous of the beauty of a mortal named Psychē, Aphrodite sent Eros on a mission to make her fall in love with an ugly man. Upon seeing Psychē for the first time, Eros was so distracted by her beauty he accidentally pricked himself with the arrow intended for her. And so it came to be, the god of love fell in love himself.

EROS' MESSAGE

Seeking a relationship as an avoidance mechanism is different from combining a connection with another individual alongside inner work. It is beneficial to be on a journey toward self-actualisation, awareness and self-soothing before entering a relationship; however, that doesn't mean you have to be at a place of completion. An intention set in motion matched with the growth relationships offer can be ideal. There is beauty to be found in remaining single, as there is through relationships.

The remedy to certain wounds and meeting certain needs require elements plentiful in relationships, as some of these are inherently challenging to address in isolation. Some scars remain dormant until a trigger draws them to the surface, ready to be released and soothed. A relationship offers the environment for this.

If you have an avoidant or anxious attachment style, working toward having a secure attachment occurs through learning via interaction. Hyper-independence can be overcome by slowly easing into receptivity with a partner. Fears of intimacy can be healed through being intimate. Fears of vulnerability can be healed through being vulnerable with a partner. Fears of rejection and abandonment can be healed by opening your heart to another. Sexuality can be liberated through opening up sexually with a lover. Of course, only do these things when you feel ready and safe.

Learning how to communicate effectively arises from difficult conversations and conflict resolution. Developing empathy and understanding comes from learning about another person's idiosyncrasies, patterns and ways of thinking.

You do not need to love yourself 100 percent to be loved and to love another. Embracing self-love can be mirrored through the love another provides you with, and you can learn how to give yourself love by seeing how you give it to a partner. Make it a goal to lavish yourself in love as grandly as you do your partner instead of giving love to get love.

You can be in a relationship as you are now, even with parts of your life not fully figured out. Be on the journey of self-love and healing so that you are not relying on another to make you feel happy and whole; however, remain open to love.

GANESHA

*The problems you are facing have solutions.
Step into the role of leader and use your power
to overcome your obstacles with logic and
transformational power.*

Elephant-headed Ganesha is the Hindu god of beginnings, good fortune and success. Known as the remover of obstacles, his father is Shiva, the god of creation, and his mother is Parvati, a fertility goddess. Translating to 'Lord of the People' in Sanskrit, Ganesha is one of the most beloved deities in Vedic culture and is called upon by many to aid in bringing opportunities and prosperity. The origin of Ganesha's elephant head traces back to a dispute between his parents. During bath time, Parvati asked Ganesha to guard the door. Taking his directive very seriously, he stood firm as Shiva tried to enter. Angered at the insubordinate behaviour, Shiva decapitates him, promptly replacing his head with that of an elephant. The god of beginnings, Ganesha places obstacles across the path of those on a new venture. Ganesha understands that the skills and resilience acquired from overcoming obstacles will play a role in shaping future prosperity and success.

GANESHA'S MESSAGE

Look at the challenges that cross your path as opportunities in disguise. A crisis initiates a new phase, readying you to release the old and fortify the new. Obstacles arise to provide chances to create. Use them as a springboard to bounce into more powerful timelines. Problem-solving is evolution in action.

Attempting to have a life void of problems can be a problem in itself. Avoidance is an issue that leads to keeping yourself small. Are you evading things because you don't feel capable of confronting them? Side-stepping problems breeds a monotonous existence with no resilience developed, contrast experienced or critical thinking to exercise the brain.

Your challenges are your natural fodder for growth. Humans are innately wired to use them as evolutionary tools. Just as our ancestors learned to solve their problems—and thus developed society as we now know it to be—you can do the same.

Civilisation is a series of constructions born from a string of issues faced by those who walked before us. The advancement of our biological evolution, inventions and technology all derived from problems solved. Houses were created from the issues associated with no shelter. Heating, cooking, clothing, medical and technological advancements all result from a need. We now reap the advantages of the solutions born from the past and continue to use those past inventions as launchpads for further growth.

It's not about being compliant with the negative in your life but embracing the undesirable to utilise in elevating your circumstances. This is the difference between letting life happen to you and mastering your ability to manipulate energy as the Magician archetype in the tarot.

No matter which route you opt to take, there will be a unique set of complications presented to you to overcome. Starting a family will come with tribulations and stress, as will starting a business or university course, writing a book or any other goal you aspire to achieve. Instead of trying to avoid a life free of problems, design a life that brings problems with it that you feel are worth having. You will still have problems, because they are inevitable — but at least you will enjoy the ones you have more when they are linked to the life you want.

GEB

*Life is your canvas, and you are the creator.
Find purpose in joy, not obligation, and embrace
the transformative power of living authentically
and with creative intent.*

A chief figure in the origin story of ancient Egypt, Geb is the god of the earth and the father of snakes. With an affinity for earth magic, he created the landforms on Earth and possessed the ability to control them. A member of the Great Ennead—nine deities worshipped in Heliopolis—Geb is the son of Shu (the god of air) and Tefnut (the goddess of moisture). As the twin of

Nut, the goddess of the sky, the pair were born tightly gripping each other's arms, representing the relationship between the earth and sky, with air being the only separation between the two. Geb's laughter is believed to be so powerful it creates earthquakes and helps the crops grow.

GEB'S MESSAGE

Life is a blank slate; the meaning you construct produces significance. Creator gods can make whatever they decide to. The landforms created can look however the god pleases; there are no set rules. And *you* are a creator in your own right. You do not need to strive towards a destined purpose. You don't have to *find* your purpose, you get to create it. Create with the power of your joy and laughter, not from a sense of 'should'. Rather than tick a set of boxes on a checklist created for you, decide what you want on that checklist.

Life means whatever you decide it means. You do not have to prove anything to anyone, not even to yourself. Simply being here and experiencing is your overarching purpose. You don't need to single-handedly solve all the world's problems. You are one person amongst billions. Release the pressure atop your shoulders.

If you want to impact the world, do so by simply enjoying yourself. The more people living in a content, open-hearted space, the better. A simple life such as meditating on the beach, gardening or reading by the fire at night can be more transformative for the world than working hard at a goal you have decided makes you worthy. Over-productivity because you don't feel worthy or enough leaves you feeling stressed and hollow. Find purpose because it incites excitement, joy or peace from deep within, not as a marker of your worth.

Spread light wherever you are. A spiritual career is not the only way to bring forth change. Impactful people are needed everywhere — in all professions and walks of life. Many careers reach people in times of need. The work you enjoy doing is a worthy way of spending time. The skills accrued thus far, whether time management, customer service skills, sales or as a caregiver, can be transferred to more fulfilling work. Things you had a latent talent for or were naturally drawn to as a child can also indicate purpose.

Seek purpose out of wonderment, not duty. There's nothing you are obligated to do. Do what you feel would be great rather than what you think is laid out for you. You don't have to figure out what the Universe wants you to do — you are a part of it. You are a segment experiencing itself in the physical. Exert your creative will.

You don't have to stumble across your one destined mission. It can be many small things wending on a path — one workshop segueing into a string of events leading to a full repertoire. There is insurmountable power to be found by living immersed in your purpose. Instead of feeling adrift, you will feel momentum driving you toward a meaningful future.

HERCULES

*You are strong, not always by choice,
but sometimes because you had to be.
You are moving toward a horizon where
you will be safe to be held and nurtured.*

Central to Roman and Greek mythology, Hercules—also known as Heracles—is a demi-god treasured for his strength. Viewed as a hero, Hercules was sired from an illicit love affair between Zeus and Alcmene, a mortal princess. Demonstrating his superhuman abilities from the beginning of his life, he strangled two snakes sent to kill him by Hera, furious at her husband's infidelity. Growing up with many incredible mentors, Hercules had outgrown them in strength before adulthood. He grew up to accomplish many admirable feats, one of the most notorious being 'the twelve labours', which included tasks he completed while under the rule of his cousin, King Eurystheus.

HERCULES' MESSAGE

Understandably, you are tired of being tough. The harshness of life can leave you feeling in desperate need of some gentleness and nurturing. Life can leave you feeling like you've just battled out the twelve labours of Hercules. Developing strength and resilience as attributes will take you far. However, sometimes it gets tiring.

Strength borne from survival differs from the strength you have chosen to exhibit. Decisions made from forced strength are not always in your best interest. Feeling like you are strong enough to be the bigger person or to take on the role of forgiving and teaching is not always the road to growth and does not always benefit you. Putting your comfort aside to make another person comfortable does not serve you.

It's exhausting to hear that you're strong when you'd rather not be, yet you've had to be, especially when you're barely holding on. This can leave you feeling invalidated and unseen. Remaining sturdy when life throws you losses and curveballs vastly differs from the strength required to overcome fears and create new things. A time will come when you can apply your resilience to endeavours worth it to you — for your gain, not survival. Reach out to support networks available to you. Reaching out takes pluck, as does asking for help and being open about your feelings, vulnerabilities and mistakes.

You do not have to be unwaveringly tough. You do not have to do everything alone. You are allowed to admit you are hurt. You are allowed to cry. Even if you think crying won't fix anything, it still holds value — it purges the old, cleanses and validates you. It may not solve all your problems, but it's not meant to. The emotional release brings cleansing, clarity and respite from stoic steadfastness. Sometimes, it takes breaking down the rigid exterior walls to have a revelation. Temporarily allowing the pillars of strength to crumble will give you the renewal necessary to create new, fortified foundations.

You have the fortitude to keep going; you can conquer every problem you face and have moments of vulnerability before you feel your strength recoup.

HERMES

Have that difficult conversation. Rather than avoiding conflict, face it head-on with open and transparent deliberation for richer connections.

The messenger of the gods, Hermes is a herald and a god playing an essential role in Greek mythology. Born from a powerful ancestry, his parents were Zeus and the goddess of nymphs, Maia. His other most well-known role is that of a psychopomp—a guide of souls—who would escort the dead to the god of the Underworld, Hades. Equally, Hermes is a god and trickster, a patron of good luck and of thieves. His myths include learning to hunt from the goddess Artemis, slaying the hundred-eyed giant Argus Panoptes and guiding Persephone back to her mother, Demeter, when Hades abducted her. He is well-known for being the divine messenger and inventing speech. With his winged sandals, Hermes would travel between the gods and mortals to communicate important messages between them.

HERMES' MESSAGE

Is avoiding the temporary discomfort of a difficult conversation worth giving up the opportunity to speak your mind? Consider the nights you may spend going over and over the points related to the issue because they were never released. It is best to speak up at the time and get the weight off your chest. Develop your inner messenger archetype and become efficient at healthy communication and necessary conflict resolution.

Conflict is a component of healthy relationships. Instead of letting unresolved issues fester and manifest toxicity later, communicate openly and appropriately now. The longer annoyances, grievances and ill feelings are kept muffled, the more likely they will break down your relationships over time. Looming in the background, replaying in your mind and becoming expressed through passive-aggressive behaviours will eventually wear down even the strongest bond. Confront things head-on in a calm yet clear manner.

Lessons in detachment, letting go, boundaries and prioritising peace are prevalent on a spiritual path. Learning how to healthily resolve conflict and make amends is also imperative. Instead of cutting people out at the first sign of opposition, a difficult conversation can do wonders for the long term.

When someone you love is willing to put themselves in an uncomfortable position to bring up an issue to resolve, consider that they want a clear, open relationship with you that prospers moving forward. Airing everything out gives a chance to release anything that could cause hostility. Talking out grievances can bring clarity, new perspectives and resolution. Discussing complicated topics and arriving at a better place develops closeness and deepens trust.

Acquire conflict resolution skills to employ in your personal and professional relationships. Implement communication skills, such as using 'I feel' statements rather than 'you did' statements or using 'compliment sandwiches' — starting and ending with a positive statement, with the confronting information in the middle. Opt for in-person communication to avoid losing subtext conveyed through tone, eye contact and body language. It is easy to misconstrue the energy behind a message via text as it often appears harsher without the nonverbal cues face-to-face offers.

Focus on conscious communication, and you will find clarity, strengthened bonds and a mind at peace. The quality of your communication will influence the quality of how you relate with another person. Using these techniques (and more) will lead to greater understanding and increase the closeness between you.

HIAWATHA

The antidote to isolation and loneliness is available through building ample platonic connections. Focus on building a solid community to foster intimacy and support.

History remembers the Native American leader, Hiawatha, as a precolonial sage from the 12th century. His name means 'he who combs'. Hiawatha was a Mohawk or Onondaga chief known for his speaking skills and messages of peace. He became the representative for Dekanawidah ('Great peacemaker'), helping this prophet and spiritual leader compose the *Great Law of*

Peace and the *Peace Hymn*, recorded on ancient wampum belts. Because Dekanawidah had a speech impediment, he helped teach the prophet's belief that peace was to be found through a unified nation of tribes, having faith that it was possible to end suffering and warfare brought on by the division of his people. Hiawatha is regarded reverently for his role in unifying the Seneca, Cayuga, Onondaga, Oneida and Mohawk. The Haudenosaunee (Iroquois) League was established through his dedication to unifying the people.

HIAWATHA'S MESSAGE

You are but one drop in the ocean that is humankind. It is becoming more common for people to feel isolated or like outsiders. If you have felt either of these things, it is time to focus on fostering a sense of unity with others to cloak you in the sense of belonging.

As society converts to online communication, we are prone to isolation more than ever. We are shifting away from a communal living design toward an individualistic one. Evolution has designed us to be social creatures, so these modern changes shouldn't take that away from us. From both spiritual and biological standpoints, community benefits you greatly.

Emphasise the platonic relationships in your life. While romantic relationships can play a special role, platonic relationships can bring you the love of a lifetime. Platonic love delivers purity and depth outside of the qualities of romantic love. Building these up can be a source more profound than even the most beautiful stories between lovers.

Developing a community where you can share intimacy and resources and provide giving and receiving will award you with enrichment. Nurturing platonic relationships requires going deeper than the surface. Small talk and surface-level relating have their place, but showing up with vulnerability, depth and 'masks off' creates a genuine sense of community.

If you struggle with holding space and being receptive to having space held for you, focus on *presence*. You don't always require the right words or solutions; just being there is often what people need. Instead of coming up with the perfect sage advice, focus on being caring and supportive. People won't necessarily remember the exact words you had to offer; however, they will remember feeling seen, validated and cared for. That is what is important.

To assist in finding a sense of belonging, look for local meetups for topics you are interested in. Join a book club, take up workshops on interesting topics, take up a group sport or be the person to organise family events or get-togethers with friends and like-minded people. Be the one to bring others together to feel the blessing of a community surrounding you. The sense of community you build will help you feel safe, supported and at ease in the world.

HORUS

Do it your way. Shirk the narrative other people have created for your life. Retrieve the past for healing. Your story belongs to you, and so do your choices.

Appearing as a falcon, or falcon-headed, Horus is the ancient Egyptian god of kingship and the sky and ruler of the air. As god of the sky, his right eye was the sun—symbolising power—and his left eye was the moon, representing healing. When his father, Osiris, was brutally murdered by Seth, Horus was magically conceived by his mother, Isis. Isis withdrew to the banks of the

Nile Delta to give birth to her son, intending to raise him with the purpose of avenging his father's death. Horus' childhood years were spent in seclusion and preparation for battle. His birth was overshadowed by the loss of his father, and so he had many expectations thrust upon him. Eventually, it all led to the battle against his uncle. Defeating Seth, Horus lost his left eye in battle. Isis magically restored his eye, which he offered to his dead father to protect him in the afterlife. The restorative powers of the Eye of Horus became a symbol of protection against evil in ancient times, continuing to be used to this day.

HORUS' MESSAGE

When contemplating the idea of the inner child, it is natural to picture your five-year-old self. However, it also represents your inner infant, inner teenager and everything in between. Tap into the aspects of your past that went through certain events and give yourself the space to release the emotions they held. Connect with the infant within who needs to be nurtured and tenderly cared for. Become reacquainted with your child self and tap into purpose, wonder and joy. Reconnect with your teenage self to draw on energies of rebellion, individuality and rage.

Your childhood provides insights into the foundation of your current self. Research Maslow's 'Hierarchy of Needs'. To what degree were your needs met according to those listed on the pyramid? Did you experience any deficiencies? Subconsciously derived beliefs of what we can receive now are relative to what we received in our formative years. Is there room to broaden the scope of what you can receive from now on and what you will eliminate from your life if it isn't up to scratch?

Unintentionally, parents may seek to satisfy unfulfilled needs by creating a family, whether from a longing for the love they missed or societal pressures. Some expect children to fulfil their unmet dreams or adhere to societal expectations, leading to unexplored ramifications in child-rearing. It's time to unravel long-held expectations that your inner child may still be carrying.

You do not have to climb onto the pedestal envisioned for you, nor do you have to step down to the limitations. You do not have to keep forcefully fitting into the boxes your parents, employers, friends and peers have constructed. Be unleashed from the role of dutiful offspring; conformity restricts your exuberance.

What do you envision for your life? How would you live without the pressure of opinion pressing down on you? Your inner child holds this insight. Inner child healing, shadow work, emotional release, and perspective shifting can exponentially change how your needs and wants can be met. You are worthy of receiving basic level care and deeply nourishing love. When you are your own person with your unique needs and wants met, you are more capable of being the noble king of your world and leading others to self-empowerment.

ITZAMNÁ

Healing is happening. Work with your physical body to gain insight into the remnants of your emotional and energetic processing.

A highly respected deity within the Mayan religion, Itzamná is acknowledged for many roles. He is the god of the sun, lord of the heavens, the east and west and the day and night. He comes from a powerful heritage — his father is the creator god, Hunab Ku. In Maya tradition, he is touted as the bringer of writing, books, knowledge and culture to his people. Not only was he the creator of writing, but he was also the inventor of Mayan medicine and calendars. He is recognised for the discovery of cultivating corn. Married to Ixchel—goddess of healing—Itzamná could rid people of fatal illnesses and heal them from disease.

ITZAMNÁ'S MESSAGE

You can heal now by integrating your mind, body and emotions. Although distinct, these elements come together, revealing areas of energy ready to be explored and pathways where energy flows effortlessly.

It is common to wonder why bad things are occurring, physical ailments still come up, and painful emotions still arise after significant healing. It can become an addiction over time to always look toward the next layer of healing, and it can come from a place of self-punishment. Healing occurs because you deserve to feel the entire functioning of your mind and body. No matter what, you are still human, and there will always be challenges to face. Healing makes you more equipped to face those challenges with the skills to triumph. Bring awareness to the energy behind your intent to further your path.

At first, dealing with repressed emotions and building emotional intelligence can be a bit like opening the floodgates to a full dam. Humans are intended to be emotional beings; unsticking your emotions and getting adept at feeling will not hinder future sentiments from occurring. It deepens your ability to do so, and you will reap the benefits of a life tuned in. As you tune in to your emotions, your mind and body will show you clues to the mysteries lurking in the past.

The body remembers what the mind does not. Your emotions and thoughts are entwined deeply with your physical body. Thoughts and feelings linked energetically to past trauma and events (in this life and past lives) can present themselves as physical ailments. As you journey forth, you will find discovery through various modalities, such as Bowen Therapy, Acupuncture or Kinesiology. Research the links between the physical, emotional and spiritual to find holistic solutions to nagging problems on every level. Once a physical ailment presents itself, a dual approach of working on the physical condition and the problem's psychosomatic root can help find relief.

In chronic illness, pain and disability, be mindful of the spiritual teachings consumed. Some teachings can lead you to feel bad about yourself for the chronic disease and for having difficulty overcoming it — some even imply you are responsible for such things. This card is here to tell you it is not your fault; you didn't do anything wrong. There can be unforeseen circumstances at play and information you are not yet privy to. This is not to say that healing is impossible, but to be gentle and patient with yourself. Moving forward on your wellness journey, simultaneously hold perspectives of hope and gentle surrender. As your story continues, you will discover the unravelling of the unknown, and support that is still to come.

JADE EMPEROR

Unresolved fears may be bubbling up inside of you. Nervousness is a part of the process that gets you out of your comfort zone, moving you toward growth. Use it to your advantage.

The Jade Emperor, or Yù Huáng, the Heavenly Grandfather, is the supreme god of Chinese folk religion. According to Taoist mythology, he is the ruler of all heavens, ruling over more than thirty gods. It began when Yù Huáng was born — a bright light emanated from him, filling up the kingdom. After a long period of meditation, he became immortal and stepped into the role of helping people with their problems. Even though he was not a god, he visited their realm, where he came across a demon who had invaded heaven and defeated the gods. Although a mortal, Yù Huáng used his wits and bravery to conquer and overcome. He worked through his human limitations to transcend through action and move forward. After winning a battle with the demon, the gods were so grateful they decided to give Yù Huáng the title of Jade Emperor, which earned him the position of supreme ruler.

JADE EMPEROR'S MESSAGE

Fear remains dormant until something triggers it. For example, you may have an underlying fear of planes, yet you won't feel that bubble up within you until you buy a plane ticket. Or, if you fear intimacy, you probably go about your day without it being an issue until things start becoming deep in a dating scenario. The core of the fear was always there, although it didn't come to the surface until you were faced with it or until it became tangible.

This is the same for things that make you feel nervous. It will take jumping out of your comfort zone and entering new heights to have nerves show themselves. As you venture out into uncharted territory, nervousness will likely be a feeling that arises within you.

When you feel like a bundle of nerves and long to hide under a blanket with all your plans cancelled, ask yourself: are you nervous or excited? Excitement and fear can present themselves physiologically in similar ways. Shifting your perspective to see that your passion and desire to be doing big things in the world is showing up as excitement will assist you in turning toward the feelings instead of running away.

Physiologically, having an adverse reaction can feel extremely uncomfortable. When you have assessed the situation at hand and feel safe to conquer your nerves, remind yourself that discomfort won't hurt you. The things that excite you are an indication of something important. Your passions are worth the effort.

People who do scary things regularly aren't fearless — they have become adept at the process. It's perfectly okay to be frightened. Just ensure you don't let it stifle the things that bring you joy. Making it a practice to do scary things will enhance your ability to show up for yourself.

Channel nervous energy into forward momentum. Leverage your automated bodily responses to your advantage, harnessing adrenaline to propel you toward your passion. Excitement is good. Achieving something you didn't think you could is fantastic, and it leads you to feel more confident and comfortable in your own skin. The more you do this, the greater sense of sovereignty you will experience.

JANUS

You carry your past and future selves within. You are the healer for the past version of you, and your future self is the spirit guide for the current you. Feel that love through time and space.

Roman myth speaks of Janus as the god of beginnings associated with doorways, life and death, and the past, present and future. Janus, the offspring of the influential god Apollo, has two faces — one facing left and the other right, allowing him to see into the past and future. Representing time, he is a symbol of transitions and the change that is available through progress.

January is the sacred month of Janus, representing the threshold of new beginnings. It is a time to look backwards and forwards just as Janus does, reflecting on the past and looking ahead to the upcoming year. Also sacred to Janus are all gateways that offer opportunities for transition.

JANUS' MESSAGE

In the darkest moments, when the brunt of the loneliness of being human in a world that can be brutal is felt, know you are not truly ever alone. The fallacy of time can lead to feeling limited and deep-seated loneliness. Surrounding yourself with the loving, nourishing care found through support systems and romantic and platonic relationships is great; however, you also have yourself.

Every time a memory surfaces, the present version of you envelops the past version of you in active memory. If the thought of this memory has occurred 15 times over the years, all these versions of you hold a different perspective and emotion while remembering. There may be multiple versions of you sprinkled throughout time and space holding space for you in that moment — maybe providing validation or even shedding tears on your behalf. In the present, a pivotal childhood moment can be a source of wisdom and perspective, shaping not only the teenager but also the 20, 30 and even 80-year-old selves, enveloping each with a comforting cloak of affirming love. You are not alone. You are seen, held and supported.

Forgive your past selves for not knowing what you know now. You did your best with the information held then; the choices made served a purpose. Change current habits to implement timeline shifts, resulting in an altering of the future. Do something today to make your past self feel secure and set up your future for success.

You are the higher self to your inner child, and your future self is a spirit guide for the current version of you. The current you is a memory for the future you. All versions are holding space right now. The 80-year-old version could be sitting and thinking of you fondly, reflecting on your bravery and resilience, and sending soothing for any pain.

When you reminisce, you provide that version of yourself with validation of experiences and love for everything. Time is stacked up on itself — the past, current and future walking hand in hand at this moment.

Reach out to the past and the future to facilitate healing and change. Returning to past events and working through unmoved emotions will shift perspectives and bring healing. Working with future versions of yourself is a reminder that there's a 'you' that has already done it. Tap into the understanding that the vision you strive to achieve already exists within a wise version of yourself. And that version of you will appreciate all the steps you are taking for them in this phase.

KRISHNA

Instead of explaining away your feelings, permit yourself to find emotional release. You are valid. A spotlight on emotional intelligence and skill will bring you harmony and grace.

Krishna is a Hindu supreme god recognised as the eighth embodiment of Vishnu — the preserver of the universe. He is associated with compassion, divine beauty, joy and love. According to Hindu mythology, Vishnu reincarnated as Krishna to defeat the evil King Kamsa. Vishnu plucked two hairs—one dark and one white—from his head. He placed the dark strand within the womb of the goddess Devaki, the king's sister, thus creating Krishna. The white hair created Krishna's older brother. Born from the dark strand, Krishna became known as 'The Dark One'. After many trials and tribulations, Krishna ultimately achieved the aim of his incarnation, defeating his uncle. A huntsman—mistaking Krishna for a deer—accidentally shot him in his one weak spot, his heel. Showing immense emotional intelligence, he expressed love and compassion to the hunter, resulting in his ascension back to heaven upon his death.

KRISHNA'S MESSAGE

A stark reality is that many people don't know how to feel. Instead of being taught emotional literacy, many grew up encouraged to switch off. Now, we have a society of adults starting from scratch.

To begin, strip it back to the bare basics. Implementing a fundamental level of daily emotional evaluation will help you out of repression, distraction, emptiness and numbness. The emotional realm exists outside the mental realm and thinking can impede feeling, but first, conceptual development of emotional intelligence must occur.

Print out a 'feelings wheel' and stick it to the front of an exercise book. Daily, take this book and write 'I feel …' and journal what comes to mind. At first, you might not know, and that's okay. Putting pen to paper and getting out even one word is a start.

On your feelings wheel, the first ring will have some simple feelings words such as 'good, sad, bad', etc. Write down one of these words and look to the next ring listing more nuanced feelings under that initial umbrella word. Write 'I feel this because ...', and once you have that answer, repeat 'I feel this because ...', going five layers deep to reach the core.

This task is not to continue a habit of thinking about your feelings but rather to assist you in becoming aware of your emotional body instead of feeling empty, numb and out of touch. Once you start efficiently identifying your emotions, practise processing them.

Now, it's time to feel. Get comfortable with being uncomfortable. Sitting in discomfort will assist you in resisting the urge to push it back down. Take deep breaths, and instead of providing logic for the emotion, feel it physically. Rather than explaining it away or using logic to escape it, breathe into it and feel the physical sensation within your body.

When you experience painful emotions, you are shown the tremendous depth of your capacity to feel. The degree to which you can feel pain is the same degree to which you can feel ecstasy. Shutting off pain closes you down to everything else on the spectrum of experience.

As you develop your emotional intelligence and apply your knowledge to grow your skills, you will experience clarity and cleansing. As a result, your joy will become sharper, and your ability to exhibit compassion, love and empathy will be stronger.

LOKI

Wisdom can be attained through even the most absurd of life's trials. Life brings you experiences in a multitude of forms. Learn, grow and laugh through them all, even the chaos.

Norse trickster Loki is the god of mischief known as the Father of Lies. Loki was a member of the Æsir — the principal pantheon in Norse mythology. Loki sired three horrible children with the giantess Angrboða — Fenrir, a wolf; Jörmungandr, a sea serpent; and Hel, the goddess of death. All three of his children were involved in Ragnarök — a series of events that included a battle ending in the death of the gods. Cunning and morally ambiguous, Loki would sometimes stir up mischief and other times offer wise counsel and lessons through his trickery. He used his ability to shapeshift and change his gender to play out his troublemaking and create discord and mischievous lessons amongst his fellow gods.

LOKI'S MESSAGE

Chaos can sneak up on you like an annoying trickster crossing your path. Sometimes, you can feel tricked by the universe — like signs which led you to believe something was for you but led you to a different experience. Not because you were destined to keep the thing but because it was an integral, yet temporary, part of your larger story. The way to prevent the trickster energy from taking your power is by finding the joy in every situation.

Trickster energies can be in your best interest, either redirecting you, assisting your growth or leading you toward laughing through the absurdity. Instead of thinking, "Why is this happening again?" use this as a chance to gauge how far you have come and consider how you will react if this pops up on your path again.

To find the enticing allure in life that you may have missed, consider that your learning is not tied to a pass or fail grade. Look through the lens of wonder in a passionate, curiosity-quenching manner rather than one akin to studying all night for a stressful maths quiz. You will be more inclined to follow a path that entices you rather than what you think you should do.

If you decide your situation is a test, it is. If you decide it is a lesson, it is. If you conclude it happened because you're not good enough, that is the meaning that will be constructed in your reality. Only you can determine what your prior experiences mean and what you can make of your current circumstances.

You are here to experience, not to accomplish. Accomplishment may be one of the experiences you are here for, yet it is not the be-all and end-all of earthly life. The idea that you're here to be tested can lead to a mindset of not being enough as is. It creates a harsh environment.

Reframe the human journey so that it's about your soul understanding what it feels like to have a physical experience. This sets you up for less pressure. You will learn and grow as you experience physical existence without beating yourself up for 'failing tests' and not being enough. With the pressure alleviated, you will remember that life can be fun, not a chore, and you can tap into joy on a level not yet experienced.

LUGH

Allow waves of grief to wash over you. Pain from loss and betrayal needs time, space and support for healing. Rather than denying your pain, face it with tenderness.

In Celtic lore, Lugh is the god of justice and the leader of the Tuatha Dé Danann — Gaelic for 'people of the goddess Danu'. Lugh is associated with oath keeping, the sun and thunderstorms, and is the father of Ireland's most legendary hero, Cú Chulainn. Under the rule of Lugh, the Tuatha Dé Danann won the victory against a race of violent giants called the Fomorians. Lugh's father, Cian, was savagely killed by three brothers — Brian, Iuchair and Iucharba. Overcome with grief and rage, Lugh sets out to enact revenge. Achieving his desire to end the lives of his father's murderers, Lugh acquires his legendary magical spear, Gáe Assail, and his hound, Failinis.

LUGH'S MESSAGE

The moment grief first hits you is an impact like no other. It brings you to your knees, knocking the wind out of your lungs. Grief is said to be stored in and processed via the lungs, making breathing difficult when you first feel the impact of loss. The grieving process requires a range of physiological and mental responses. It is an unpredictable roller coaster taking you on unexpected twists and turns; process what is coming up as it comes up.

Understanding the five stages of grief—denial, anger, bargaining, depression and acceptance—helps you enter into flow instead of fighting the inevitable. When loss hits you, your brain goes into a state of denial to assist your body with the shock. You may experience an inability to tap into emotion or tears, or you may feel numb. This is not a time for guilt or shame for avoiding your feelings; your body protects you.

When anger (or another painful emotion) eventually presents itself, find healthy outlets to release it. Whether it is slow burning or quick to rise, release it with conscious intention. Scream into a pillow, smash some tennis balls against a brick wall, or write out whatever you think and feel and then burn it.

The next phase is bargaining — thinking of what you could have done differently or could do differently to stop the loss from happening. This is followed by a stage of depression leading you to alone time where processing can occur; make sure you don't withdraw to an unhealthy level. Although you will never be okay with a huge loss occurring, you will reach a degree of acceptance. It is natural to loop back to grief in the future to shed a deeper layer. The stages of grief do not occur linearly — they zig and zag.

Mourning the death of a loved one, the loss of a relationship, friendship or a desired future you envisioned takes you on an overwhelming journey of pain, release and rebuilding. It will take time, grit, determination, support and patience. When you are in the midst of grief, trust the process, knowing you will enter a phase of acceptance in due time. When you emerge from the depths of grief processing, you will be able to take a recalibrating breath deep into your lungs, filling you back up with vitality. You will venture back into the world, seeing the vibrancy return around you.

MAUI

This is an invitation to take baby steps toward breaking down habits that no longer serve you. When you are creating a new habit, each step compounds to make an extreme change later.

Myths of the gregarious Polynesian legend of Maui span across Hawai'i and New Zealand. He is also referred to as 'Maui of a Thousand Tricks' due to the expansiveness of his exploits and the vast number of tales about him. Regarded as a hero and notorious for being a trickster, Maui sometimes resorted to mean ruses, yet at other times, he decided to use his intellect for good. Born prematurely and thinking he was dead, his mother cast him into the ocean wrapped in a tuft of her hair. Rescued by Tana—the sky god—Maui is attributed with the remarkable feat of creating the Polynesian islands and for tricking Mahuika—the fire goddess—into gifting humanity fire.

MAUI'S MESSAGE

Transformation requires actively shifting your current reality. By changing your routines, you can turn toward the direction you prefer. You can become so accustomed to your existing systems that it's similar to floating downstream, dragged along by the current. Breaking a habit and creating a new one entails becoming aware and consciously turning in a different direction with your paddle. Bringing awareness to your daily routines is more uncomfortable than going along your natural trajectory of repetition. Decide which habits still serve you, which you want to break and which you wish to form.

Just as Maui had to decide moment to moment whether to partake in trickster pranks or demigod-level creations, you have to choose which path to take when each is presented to you. The choice is yours. Building the strength needed to create beautiful things happens slowly over time. Every seemingly small decision forms a new habit, gradually compounding to pave the way to greatness.

A habit is an intention set in motion. Go slowly, breaking and creating one little step at a time. The ripple effect beginning from one action will flow out with impact. Sticking to your new patterns is easier when coming from a place of gentleness and empowerment rather than self-degradation. Break it down to one choice at a time rather than thinking about all of your future actions. When breaking the habit of drinking five coffees a day, take it one coffee at a time. Think to yourself, "This one choice right now is taking me on a timeline that benefits my future self. This one shift of timeline will alter my course."

It becomes easier to repeat that little step once you've done it the first time. Make it as simple as possible. You don't need to torture yourself and make dramatic shifts instantly. Sometimes, we overestimate the change we can make in one month yet underestimate the progress we can make in a year. A five-minute walk today can build to a daily hour walk down the track.

Another way to make your progress gentler is to have an alternative, healthier replacement that comforts you. Rather than forgoing comfort and coping mechanisms to transform, figure out what higher-order need your old habit provides and find a way to bring that in. For example, replace your coffee with piping hot tea instead of restricting it to nothing. Design a list of healthy coping mechanisms to turn to when needed. Modify your current timeline by making small decisions to support the future version of you and feel the transformative power you hold come bursting forth in giant waves.

MELCHIZEDEK

Seek wisdom from a mentor to open new gateways to your soul. Teach and share your knowledge, for as you teach, you learn on a deeper level.

Melchizedek, meaning 'my king is righteousness' in Canaanite, is remembered as not only the king of Salem but also the first-ever priest. He was the first person to be referred to with the title *'kohen'* (priest) in the Bible. Written about in the Old and New Testaments, Melchizedek is revered so strongly that Abraham—the first Hebrew patriarch—offered to pay him tithes, demonstrating the magnitude of his importance. Yeshua (also known as Jesus) held the title of High Priest in the order of Melchizedek, according to the New Testament's *Epistle to the Hebrews*. Other important biblical figures who were initiated into the priesthood of Melchizedek include Moses, Elijah and Isaiah.

MELCHIZEDEK'S MESSAGE

It is time to focus on learning something new. Seeking a mentor will assist in elevating you to a new level. Hidden pieces of wisdom dormant within you will be unlocked, awaiting the right time and conditions to bloom. With this newfound understanding, you will be ushered onto a path of higher passion and illuminated truths. A mentor can help you bridge the zone of proximal development — the space between what you can learn unassisted and what you can achieve with educational support.

Remember that your mentors are human and pass on the accumulated teachings learned first-hand on their wending journey. It is all too easy to get carried away with a new, exciting topic. Take the time to consider all sides, not just the source you are most drawn to. Cognitive bias can take hold and become deeply rooted, limiting your path to higher learning.

Cognitive bias is a process that occurs where people become biased toward one subjective reality, forgoing logical reasoning. Humans tend to filter information through the lens of personal preference and prior experience. To combat this, consume teachings that convey the opposite beliefs you initially held about a topic. If you still hold the same views upon researching all viable theories, at least you know you have kept an open mind to all possibilities. Knowledge is power, and so is the humility to know that there will always be more to learn and information that humans are not privy to.

As learning and teaching are two sides of the same coin, consider sharing your insights via the teaching modalities that feel right to you to expand your wisdom. The role of a teacher is to help plant seeds. If that seed is meant for the student, it will sprout roots and grow branches. If not, it won't.

You may have an important topic for you to share to accomplish your teaching journey. Yet, you will come across certain students to whom your message will not apply. That may be because it does not pertain to their purpose, soul contracts and lessons for this life, or perhaps it will plant a small seed that will sprout in years to come.

Each person has a unique path to walk. Walk yours authentically, and the people aligned with your learning and teaching will come. Your own knowledge will deepen and grow, and you will feel the deep fulfilment that comes from nourishing the seed of wisdom ready to sprout within others.

MIDAS

Gently consider where you are choosing to prioritise your valuable time and energy. When pursuing a desire, the chase is often more about the experience or emotion than the actual attainment of the object itself.

In Greek mythology, Midas, the King of Phrygia (what is now central Turkey), is most remembered for his 'Midas touch', a phrase still used colloquially. The story goes that Dionysus granted Midas a wish after saving his mentor, Silenus. Midas, not known for his intellect, requested that everything he touched would turn to gold. He soon realised his power was not limited to turning items to gold only when desired, but absolutely anything he laid his hands on, including food. The last straw was when he accidentally turned his daughter, whom he adored, into a lifeless golden statue. Not wanting to live a life barren of the soft touch of another, he begged Dionysus to take his gift back.

MIDAS' MESSAGE

Sometimes, the only thing worse than your dreams not coming true is for them to come true with unexpected or undesirable consequences. When based on distorted desire, the pursuit of happiness can be ineffectual. Attainment without self-actualisation can leave you feeling trapped in a gilded cage of your own making. Strive to build a life you are content with based on the daily functioning of your reality. Then, when the big things happen, and they don't fix all your problems, it won't be a massive letdown.

What is often conceptualised as happiness can be described as joy. Joy is a temporary peaking of elation, which can feel even more noticeable when shared with contrasting emotions. If you were in constant joy, elation would no longer be a peak; it would no longer feel as good. Good feelings fluctuate, and that's okay. Pursue happiness while also considering if you are trying to bypass other emotions.

Ironically, the act of pursuing happiness can be a negative experience. Fearing the negative is limiting; trying to escape and run toward the positive is a form of resistance. Not being afraid when the negative arises is a generative experience. When you find satisfaction in the mundane, you can chase the marvellous.

Relish in small daily pleasures and routines that feel good to you. People often desire things because they think they will give them a certain feeling or fill a hole in their lives. Sometimes, it's not really about attaining a desire or a goal that people are striving for — it's the way they think it will make them feel once they get it. When you pin all your happiness on receiving something, you may get it and realise it hasn't transformed all your shadow into gold. When the arrival of a manifestation doesn't bring the expected ecstatic joy, it is incredibly disappointing. Work on the underlying shadow. Arriving at a state of contentment outside of big life wins will help you enjoy those moments more when they arrive. Instead of having them be the escape from difficult emotions, they can be a lovely addition to an inner world that has already received careful attention.

Being content does not mean you stop desiring change and no longer have goals to strive towards. Enjoy the process, and don't connect your happiness to the outcome. The journey will feel so fruitful and rewarding that the outcome will be the cherry on top of an already awesome sundae.

NARCISSUS

Slather yourself with self-love to keep the opinion of others from hurting you. Constructive criticism will no longer feel like an attack when you allow your flaws to be seen in the light.

The myth of Narcissus arises from ancient Greece and tells the tale of an astoundingly handsome man who falls in love with himself. Narcissus was renowned for his beauty, born from a river god named Cephissu and a nymph called Liriope. It was prophesied to Liriope that her son would reach old age only if he never recognised himself. A hunter from the ancient Greek city Thespiae, Narcissus rejected all the romantic advances with which he was inundated. One day, he was wistfully staring at his reflection and became besotted with what he saw. Becoming so obsessed with his image, Narcissus lived out the rest of his days right there by the river, never taking his eyes off himself.

NARCISSUS' MESSAGE

Pride has a rightful place in your life. However, a shadow side exists, too. The thought of making self-love a priority can be intimidating because it can be correlated with narcissism. The two are very different.

Narcissism presents as grandiose self-importance but can be derived from a lack of self-esteem and self-love. Narcissism demands adoration and validation, overcompensating for a lack of inner assuredness and confidence. One does not feel enough as is, so they draw in confirmation for showy importance. They cannot see beyond themself.

Self-love is bridging that gap; self-love is radically accepting oneself as is. It is accepting the seemingly most unlovable parts of oneself. It is having confidence that does not seek out energy from others. When you have the self-love to ensure your needs and boundaries are met, you can see beyond just yourself. Self-love is having pride, while narcissism is remaining prideful, the shadow side of pride.

Remaining in the shadow side of pride can keep you from cultivating and maintaining close connections with others. Arrogance in excess keeps you from taking accountability. It prevents the ability to have tough conversations that require apologies from you, openness, kindness and understanding. Superiority is seen in black and white and doesn't allow people to mess up, including oneself. It is easier to keep a blind eye to your own mistakes and to see only the failings in others without seeing their humanity and the nuance that most situations have.

When other people exhibit conceitful qualities, do your best not to take it personally, and remember, inside of them is an inner child that doesn't feel safe and doesn't feel enough without the 'show'. If you can see prideful qualities within yourself, prioritise radical self-love and self-acceptance. Once you learn to be your own best friend in a nurturing, loving and supportive manner, it is safe to see your flaws without hatred.

Accept yourself wholly and be assertive in who you are as is. Healthy self-love will become your solace. You will create so much inner security that you will no longer feel shaken when you receive constructive criticism or an extension of an offer for deep communication. Instead of feeling unsupported, victimised and betrayed, you will have such inner calm that you don't feel as unsafe from the actions of others.

OBATALA

Extend kindness and understanding to yourself and others. The path of humanity is not an easy undertaking. See through the pain and apply the salve of love.

Within the Yoruba pantheon of West Africa, Obatala is a primordial *orisha* — spirits referred to as deities or avatars of the supreme being Olódùmarè. Obatala, which means 'king who wears white cloth', is the god of purity. He is also called Alabalase, meaning 'he who has divine authority'. According to some *pataki*—Yoruban mythological stories—he created humans using Olódùmarè's breath. Obatala is referenced as Sky Father and the father of all orishas and humankind. Husband to Yemoja, the river goddess, Obatala is admired for his kindness, compassion and peace. His sacred colour is white, and his symbol is the dove, which is associated with peace, jasmine flowers and his white crown.

OBATALA'S MESSAGE

Kindness requires immense strength, wisdom, intelligence and skill — the strength to respond instead of react, the wisdom to have emotional maturity, the intelligence to know why people are the way they are and the skill to combine these forces. Kindness is a decision to intentionally put these elements into practice in the face of adversity.

A cornerstone of this process is understanding. To comprehend the challenges that humans encounter, delve into the biological and psychological factors propelling them, and explore the historical roots behind it all. Use understanding as a means of self-love rather than it being a detriment. Being sympathetic to the pain and confusion the human condition causes can help you see that bad behaviour directed at you does not reflect your worthiness or lovability. It isn't a deficiency in you. However, it's still no excuse for the behaviour, and understanding is not a tool to condone it or stick around for more mistreatment.

Kindness doesn't necessitate enduring unpleasant situations merely for the sake of being nice. On the contrary, genuine compassion and understanding grant you clarity instead of blind ignorance. It involves recognising, with compassionate wisdom, when someone may lack the capacity to make better choices.

Open-minded benevolence allows you to love from afar. Especially when you match kindness to others with equal amounts to yourself. Practising within helps you extend it outward. To transform your self-treatment, take note of times you speak to yourself with negative self-talk. Ask yourself, "If that was my best friend, how would I have spoken to them in the same situation?" How would you want a friend to speak to you at that moment? Then, put that positive self-talk into practice, even if it feels silly or forced.

'Nice' does not always feel kind. Kindness requires honesty, whereas nice can be a fake mask worn to gain approval from another. It can be uncomfortable to be kind. Hearing the truth face to face rather than being nice just to be liked can strengthen bonds.

A caveat with honesty is to ensure it is matched with the right timing and gentleness. Delivered with tact and understanding makes honesty kind; delivered with judgment and brutality does not.

Consider the timing of your words; unsolicited advice can be perceived as criticism in the wrong circumstance. Honesty delivered with compassionate wisdom is key to keeping your bonds based in truth and closeness, yet with a feeling of safety and mutual respect.

OCASTA

Clinging on to an expected outcome may be causing you mental anguish. The expectations you place on others and the ones you allow to be placed on yourself can hold you back.

In the tradition of the Native American Cherokee Nation, Ocasta is a god of knowledge sent to help humanity on behalf of the creator deity, Unetlanvhi. He is also known as Stonecoat, referring to his coat made of flint. Unable to decide if he was good or bad, he would sway between causing chaos and doing good. When the good and bad wolves within him battled it out, he would occasionally allow one to emerge while other times making room for the other. Ocasta created witches to join him in his escapades, increasing the level of disorder he caused. They journeyed from village to village, causing all sorts of trouble in their wake. During one such visit, a group of women captured Ocasta and struck him through the heart with a stick. The men of the village cremated him, and consequently gained healing abilities, becoming the first medicine men.

OCASTA'S MESSAGE

High standards and a desire for greatness contribute to your elevation and expansion, but clinging too fiercely to expectations does not. There are three types of expectations to review your day-to-day operations: the expectation of outcomes occurring a certain way, the expectations you hold for other people, and those placed on you.

Letting go of outcomes maximises the enjoyment of your journey. Expecting love, career, friendships and finances to happen in a specific way leads to bitter disappointment, resentment and complacency. Work toward things, knowing they might not happen exactly in accordance with your plan.

Another form of expectation is painting an idea of someone in your head as a purely 'good' person and then labelling them as a 'bad' person if they make a poor decision. Expecting someone to solely be a good person puts unfair pressure on them to be perfect. Seeing all humans as flawed beings with the capacity to do bad things will keep you from a lifetime of feeling extreme reactions. If someone breaches your boundaries in such a way that you decide to remove them from your life, that is entirely reasonable; although putting people on a pedestal and condemning them as soon as they don't live up to your expectations is not.

Sometimes, we find ourselves in love with someone's potential, not the person who exists. The potential version of a person we envision in our mind is not real. People grow, transform and mature, yet it is for them only to decide if, when and in what ways that will occur. Ask yourself, "If this person were to remain exactly who they are right now, would I be okay with that?"

Review the extreme expectations you place upon yourself. Start with the ones you allow from employers, family and friends. Expectations can be put on you only if you comply. The more you exert your will, the more the people around you will get used to you living your most authentic self. Either they will get used to it, or they won't. Nonetheless, you will get used to it and will start caring less about the opinions and expectations put on you. And in turn, they will start realising that you will no longer cave to the pressure of demands of you being who they want you to be.

Let go of perfectionism and high expectations of others, and you will also free yourself. Instead of extending your precious energy to monitoring expectations, you will decide how to proceed based on how people want to show up for you. The return of the energy wrapped up in the various types of expectations will be ready to be used with relish.

ỌRÚNMÌLÀ

You are growing into your destiny. Free will and fate are working together for your highest good. Extend your free will, and divine orchestration will arrive at the right time.

For the Yoruba people of West Africa, Ọrúnmìlà is the deity who created their divination system known as Ifá. According to Yoruba mythology, he is the master diviner and high priest who possesses knowledge of the future of all humans. He is a healer and the personification of wisdom, able to sway the destiny of humans. Ọrúnmìlà was the sole observer of Olódùmarè generating the world. As the master diviner bore witness to the earth's creation, he saw each person's path, their life purpose, and even the way they would die. He communicates with people about their destinies and helps them walk their best possible path.

ỌRÚNMÌLÀ'S MESSAGE

Free will and fate move together like a summer breeze blowing through the leaves of a tree. Two separate entities merge in beautiful synchrony; the unification of the two is where magic lies.

Destiny weaves onto your path in mystical ways, showing you divine orchestration. It is not your job to make each destined moment happen. The magic is in the surprise meetings, the opportunities seemingly dropped on your path and the gobsmacking synchronicities. Merging fate and free will is having freedom in a framework.

Jumping timelines is plucking and weaving threads of fate, each one different yet just as destined as another. It was fated for the tree to grow, yet the direction in which the branches reach out was not wholly predetermined.

Each choice made is a portal to a unique timeline, thus a variant of your future. Each possible future contains events, situations, experiences and people that are fated; although different, each one is as profound as the other. Each timeline has its own destiny. If one opportunity is 'missed', another portal will open. Flexing your creative muscles and playing with different paths is your overarching destiny.

Fate is ever-changing; don't force the longevity of situations because the Universe brought it to you. The Universe doesn't work in absolutes. Destiny isn't all or nothing; it works in moments, not just forevermore. Fate is not meant to confine you. You don't have to get everything right. The free will component of life guides you to work from an open, heart-guided place, making it easier to flow toward your blueprint.

Access tools that tap into your blueprints, such as astrology, human design, numerology and tarot. The information garnered can give you glimpses of what's to come. The key themes are predestined, but how they can play out is infinite.

There is wriggle room. There is power to be found in having access to certain parts of your fate and power in the unknown aspects. Some aspects of your destiny need to play out like dominos bounding into each other without you knowing what is to come. Fate is found through hindsight, seeing the intelligence of the intricate moments webbed together to craft a majestic lifetime. Surrendering to your destiny and trusting in fate may feel counter-intuitive, but when you expect the unexpected, all things are possible.

OSIRIS

When you feel lost, self-discovery will lead you to be enchanted with life once more. Rejuvenation is found in the fertile soil left exposed amongst the vestiges of the last season.

Osiris is the ancient Egyptian god of the Underworld associated with the deceased, the afterlife and resurrection. In the vein of his creator god parents Geb and Nut, Osiris possesses plentiful power. He originated as a nature god associated with the cycle of vegetation. Over time, he shifted roles and developed his affiliations with the Underworld. He is the epitome of symbolising both death and rebirth and the cyclic nature of life. Murdered by his younger brother Seth, Osiris was resurrected by his wife Isis, who roamed Egypt distraught by his death with a powerful determination to find him. With her sister Nephthys, Isis found Osiris' scattered body parts and put them back together with her magic. With his restored life, Osiris became the ruler of the Underworld.

OSIRIS' MESSAGE

Certain phases of life guide you to points of feeling lost. There are times when you feel like you have experienced a death of one phase of life but are yet to return from the Underworld. This serves a purpose. When you venture on the journey back to yourself, you will find hidden gems you would not have unearthed without being lost in the first place. Feeling lost provides you with an opportunity to meet yourself deeper than you ever have previously. The intimate connection you will cultivate as you ponder the question, "Who am I?" will be a thing of beauty and discovery. You will find resurrection.

As you emerge from your deep excavation, you will unearth unfound enchantment. As the dust settles, look in the rubble, and you will see. This is a time to reintroduce both purpose and productivity, balanced with pleasure and freedom. Each polarity aids in the achievement of the other. Times of joy give you the energy needed to produce results you are proud of.

Seeking only pleasure can become a vice, providing hits of dopamine and escapism. To prevent this, introduce a balance of other key elements such as shadow work, community and life purpose.

The dark night of the soul and gnarly awakening or healing leads to a loss of enthrallment. In brighter times, you may have found pleasure in a variety of activities, such as reading fantasy novels, participating in team sports, playing music, spending time in nature, not having a to-do list for the day, creating art, playing video games and pursuing hobbies solely for fun rather than skill development. Collect these jewels to place gently back in your arsenal. You don't have to reinvent the wheel; indulge in simple joys.

Rebirth requires walking into the unknown, stepping onto uncharted territory without all the answers. This can be scary, yet it can be scintillating. As you allow the dust to settle after shadowy times, it is time to contemplate what is your unique expression. No more wondering what other people think; crafting an impactful life requires not caring about the opinions of others. If you want to break the mould, you can't fit into it any longer.

Ponder who you are and what you want; the answers will come. Persevere as you encounter abundant new opportunities during this time of rebirth. Dredge off the sludge, wade through the drudgery and enter a shining new cycle. Your regeneration will give you a blank slate to do as you please.

RA

Enhance your joy, abundance and play by emulating the energy of the sun. Radiance, warmth and lifeforce will bring you sustenance after a period of heaviness and release.

Ra is worshipped as one of the oldest and most important gods in ancient Egyptian mythology. A creator god and god of the sun, Ra has no parents. Instead, he was born fully developed, rising out of a lotus flower. Another version of his myth states that he rose from the benben stone — the capstone of a pyramid. The origin of life, Ra created humans from his tears. Becoming the patriarch of ancient Egyptian deities, he is the father of Shu and Tefnut, grandfather of Nut and Geb and great-grandfather of Isis, Osiris, Seth and Nephthys. To further Ra's importance to Egyptian culture, pharaohs were titled 'Sons of Ra'. Ra is not only a sun god but also the embodiment of the sun itself. The setting sun is said to be Ra travelling to the Underworld to become reborn at daybreak.

RA'S MESSAGE

On a balmy day toward the end of summer, the sun's rays hit the earth in a display of iridescent brilliance. After a swim, a man walks out of the ocean, feeling rejuvenated and livened by the warmth as he sits by the shore, basking in the light. A woman in the next neighbourhood sips her coffee; she smiles as she watches her sunflowers reach toward the sun, seeking its radiance. Next door, a young family laugh and play under a sprinkler, feeling the joy of play in the heat.

Throughout history, the sun has held various cultural roles and meanings. Its energy has predominantly been associated with masculine energy, lifeforce, abundance and vitality. The sun's blazing rays are penetrating, fierce and life-providing, a reflection of the attributes of the masculine. Honouring the sun and working with its energy will assist you in embodying these attributes, just like Ra. Not only did the ancient Egyptians praise the sun, but many other cultures have their own version of lore, origin stories and deities representing solar energy. Without the sun, we would not exist.

As the most important star in our solar system, the sun has been a life provider, light source and bringer of enlightenment. Your body undergoes vitamin D production from UV exposure (in a sun-safe manner) and the release of serotonin (a mood-boosting hormone). The sun penetrates, replenishes and warms your soul after periods of dense emotional work and release. For plants it provides sustenance through the process of photosynthesis, converting solar energy to carbon dioxide and soil nutrients into food.

Humans have always connected deeply with the sun, and it's time for you to harness your relationship with it now. Make it a habit to work with its daily cycle, and you will learn to honour your sleep, serotonin levels, energy and vitality. Working with the sun will benefit your mind, body and spirit, reminding you of your connection to lifeforce energy.

RŪAUMOKO

Awakening requires relinquishing how you have viewed truth and reality in the past. As you go through this process, allow the people around you to do so too.

Rūaumoko is a central figure in Māori mythology. He is the god of earthquakes, associated with volcanoes and the seasons. Combining the forces of his parents—Ranginui (Sky Father) and Papatūānuku (Earth Mother)—Rūaumoko is believed to be the cause of the change of seasons and responsible for all disruptions beneath the earth. Before his birth, Rūaumoko's brothers were tired of living in the dark void between their parents—the sky and the earth—and desperately desired space and sunshine. With their combined force, the brothers broke free, upsetting their parents so much that Ranginui flooded the world with his tears. While still in his mother's womb at this time, Rūaumoko tried to escape, his movements creating earthquakes for the first time.

RŪAUMOKO'S MESSAGE

'Spiritual awakening' paints a picture of softly waking up to chirping birds, wrapped in cosy blankets, ready to live a beautiful new day. It can be more akin to an obnoxious alarm forcing you out of bed from a tranquil slumber.

Whether a lovely experience or a jarring force, you can be left overwhelmed, deeply unsure of yourself and the world. Staying in a dream-like state is blissful compared to the deep excavation it takes to face the harshness of truth. To awaken, you will question the very fabric of your reality.

Spiritual awakenings are unique to the individual, sometimes coming on slowly while other times brought on by a catalytic event. A near-death experience, paranormal or psychic connection, health issues, a relationship or parenthood are some forms of catalysts. The catalyst shakes you to your core, leaving you questioning the meaning behind existence. This can be a painful experience. Awakening can feel like you—and your entire belief system—are being ripped wide open, peeled back and sometimes, scraped away.

If someone you are close to does not awaken, heal and process like you do, it doesn't mean they aren't. Feminine energy tends to awaken via intuition, receptivity and processing through discussion. Masculine energy is inclined to awaken in a somatic, visceral way through the physical body. Regardless of gender, everyone does it differently. It is important to honour the energetic processes that work for you and, on the other hand, may not work for others.

The most efficient teacher of all is experiencing for oneself. We become our own cautionary tale, learning from our past mistakes, not those of others. The more we feel the narrative of another pushed onto us, the more we want to dig our heels in to resist the pressure.

Allow others the room to figure out what their journey means to them while putting your focus back on what you value and how you choose to spend your precious time and energy. You may grow apart from some people, jobs and other elements of your life, and that's okay.

Venture forth with the freedom to awaken and grow in your unique direction, and you will find yourself surprised by how much your life changes for the better.

SHIVA

It is time to get comfortable with your failings, for they symbolise your effort. Look to failure as motivation to come up with something new. Extend your creative energy.

A Hindu deva, Shiva is the god of destruction known as 'The Destroyer'. Primarily viewed as a benevolent deity, his name means 'Auspicious One' in Sanskrit. Shiva fathered Ganesha with his wife Parvati, the mother goddess of fertility. Along with Brahma (god of creation) and Vishnu (god of preservation), Shiva is a member of the Trimurti, also referred to as the holy trinity. Although Shiva is known for destruction, he destroys to make way for the rebirth of a new cycle. He is one facet of the process of creation. Shiva destroys, Brahma (re-)creates and Vishnu preserves — each role holding equal importance in the overall picture. Vasuki—the snake depicted around Shiva's neck, coiled three times—represents the past, present and future.

SHIVA'S MESSAGE

In this photoshopped, social media-curated culture, we can be prone to showing the fruits of our success without exposure to the failures that lead to it. When you are used to seeing the best moments of the lives of those around you, it can make you feel bad about yourself when you fall short. When you see the success of others, you do not see the events that happened to lead them there. You did not see the sacrifices, faith, knocks and falls, or doubt. Similarly, when other people see your success, they may see luck where you see all the work.

Failure indicates that you have tried and taken charge and decided to attempt to do something remarkable; that is what counts. Failure is a mark of being human, and it is inevitable. It provides you with an opportunity to find another route toward success or to walk away from something no longer meant for you. It can open up a new door toward something more aligned with you. The destruction of one thing makes way for creating something brand new and perhaps even better than the last.

A failure is not complete destruction; it is just a setback preparing you for something new.

Adversity prepares you for success. It makes you resilient, teaches you what you need to know to get to the result, and turns you into a person who can handle what success will bring. Hardship makes your appetite for the result grow, providing insurmountable energy. Experiencing the negative emotions associated with failing makes the positive feelings brought by success feel even sweeter.

If you fear the impending shame of failure, think of it this way — a bit of embarrassment is better than waking up one day realising you will never know if your dreams could have come true. It is better to try and fail than look back with regret and unanswered questions. Trying is admirable and will leave you reflecting with pride for putting yourself out there and giving it a crack.

ŚUDDHODANA

Show up as a source of emotional support for others. Relinquish emotional responsibility and step into holding space for the benefit of yourself and others.

Śuddhodana, meaning 'he who grows pure rice', was the king of the Shakya people — an eastern sub-Himalayan ethnic group. Ruling with his wife, Maya Devi, Śuddhodana came to be the father of the Buddha. Maya dreamt of a son destined to be a great king or a religious leader. When his wife passed seven days after giving birth to his son, Śuddhodana, overcome with grief, became overly protective. He attempted to keep Gautama from being a religious leader by keeping his son sheltered from human suffering. He ensured Gautama remained within the confines of the palace, experiencing only pleasure and happiness.

By keeping Gautama away from the contrast pain offers pleasure, Śuddhodana pushed him toward the one thing he tried to keep him from.

ŚUDDHODANA'S MESSAGE

A first-time dad watches on nervously as his baby son takes his first steps, concerned for any stumbles and falls that may occur. Thirty years later, the same man watches his grandson take his first steps. Instead of hesitation, he now smiles, free of nerves. After watching his son's life journey, he understood that the stumbles and falls were needed to learn how to become competent at walking and then, eventually, running.

When you feel overly responsible for the emotions and journey of another, know that it is not your place to take away every possible pitfall and pain for them. You can always be a support, holding space and providing insight when you can. However, part of learning is stumbling and falling. To take away all the hardship, emotional pain and problems is to take away the growth, learning and development of resiliency.

What you think is best for someone might be the very thing that hinders their growth. Depending on a person's life path, they may need certain experiences to be a catalyst of wisdom, growth or a certain set of circumstances to send them on a particular winding path. Showing up to guide, counsel and support can be beautiful — although stepping back, relinquishing control and allowing a person to make their own choices and mistakes is essential.

The best way to become a holder of space for another person's hard times is to face your shadow. When you become sufficient at facing your darkness and sitting in discomfort, you can comfortably do the same for another without feeling drained.

Knowing that periods of darkness and difficulty serve a purpose in the bigger picture can help you not run from your own and other people's shadows. Strive toward emotional support rather than emotional responsibility, and see how you show up for yourself and others transform. You will no longer feel drained or feel a desire to control.

THOR

Instead of dwelling on your dreams, dive into deliberate actionable steps to bring them to fruition. You know what needs to be done.

In Norse lore, Thor is the god of thunder and war and is associated with agriculture, the weather and the sky. His parents are Odin, the chief of the Norse god, and Jördh, the personification of the earth. He is celebrated for his strength, courage, loyalty and honour. Thor married Sif—the goddess of harvest—and is most often depicted possessing a divine hammer called Mjölnir. He uses it as a weapon in battle to bring the dead back to life and to bring blessings. Forged by dwarfs, it can hit any target and return to him automatically. Thor travels through the nine realms in a chariot drawn by his two goats named Tanngrisnir and Tanngnjóstr. Known for his brawn, and for being headstrong, Thor often landed himself in nasty predicaments by throwing his weight around, not always with forethought. His many escapades include being captured by the giant Geirröd as he was led into a misadventure by Loki, dressing in Freyja's clothes to win back his stolen Mjölnir, and wrestling with Jörmungandr, a giant sea serpent.

THOR'S MESSAGE

Inspired action is different from action that is not based on conscious intention. It combines the heart and mind as allies working toward one goal. Inspired action requires thinking outside of the box and kicking down old paradigms. Inspired action is well thought out and planned with intention, instead of stumbling along like Thor — acting from a primal, instinctual basis, with no consideration of destination. This can be scary, although it beats living a life deemed worthy to others yet bland to yourself.

If you are waiting for the right time to strike, you may end up twiddling your thumbs forever. You are ready now; you don't need the whole plan. Strike now, lift your metaphorical Mjölnir and hit your desired target. Taking an action step will light you up like an electric bolt of lightning, firing you up, ready for more.

Your first step will lead you to the second, then the third. It is the process itself that aids in the development of your capacity to arrive at completion. Just as the caterpillar builds the strength of its future butterfly wings by making its way out of the cocoon, you will develop your resilience and test your skills through the process of action. The time for procrastinating is over.

Procrastinating can stem from a desire for perfection, but creating is messy. It's a sprawling muddle of incremental pieces draped together to become a stunning, interwoven masterpiece. Letting go of procrastinating requires you to give yourself permission to get messy and allow for failures.

Reframe failures as setbacks to create without the pressure. Get out of your own way. Start and figure out the nitty gritty as you go. It may be clunky, yet that's how you figure out what needs fine-tuning, what things you need to learn, the skills that need developing and the logistics that need addressing.

Play the long game. It takes discipline to get things done. However, your future self will reap the rewards. You may drag your feet, yet the benefits produced will be monumental.

Discipline derived from doing something you don't want to do is torture; discipline correlated with the success of your dreams is rewarding. Instant gratification has its benefits under the right circumstances. On the other hand, delayed gratification can be wildly elating.

Once you start, you might be surprised by just how ready you are. The knowledge and skills you have accumulated thus far will pour out once given the chance. Take a step, and the journey has begun.

THOTH

Your thoughts are a catalyst of transformation. Take time to think things through, deciding which thoughts you resonate with and which ones you are merely meant to observe.

The ancient Egyptian god of knowledge and wisdom, Thoth, is accredited with the invention of hieroglyphic writing and the foundation of law. He is also known as the god of magic and the moon. Some versions of his origin story describe him as being self-created at the dawn of time. Other versions tell the tale of his creation from the seed of Horus—the sky god—and born from the forehead of Seth — the god of chaos. He turned his thoughts and knowledge of the mysteries of the universe into several scrolls collectively named *The Book of Thoth* by ancient scholars. Through his creation of language and writing, he made it possible for nuggets of ideas to become fleshed-out objects, jotted down in the physical, to sprout from concept to reality. He presided over the judgement of souls in the Hall of Truth with Ma'at, goddess of truth, and Anubis, god of the dead.

THOTH'S MESSAGE

Your thoughts are a conscious cognitive process that gives insight into the totality of you. Each part of you has a voice that yearns to be heard. A thought can be a nugget of an idea, a kernel of a potential creation to grasp onto, pulling it into the physical.

Listen for these seeds of conception desiring to be drawn down into existence. With that initial thought, take one step to begin the formation. Start today, and the centrifugal motion from that step will whisk you away to unstoppable heights. Thoughts are a conduit of creation and can also indicate what needs releasing — the flipside of creation is destruction.

Not all thoughts align with who you are. Ideas arise from various aspects of you. Some come from your inner child, maternal ancestral line, paternal line or past versions of you. Others come from wounds of your psyche or indoctrinated and socialised parts of you. Some thoughts are not your ultimate truth.

Some are there simply to consider and to shine a light on your cognitive reality collected from these various places. Instead of trying to stop the thought, observe it, then bring in the new.

Trying to stop a thought leads to frustration and, consequently, more overthinking. When the momentum of your negative thoughts drags you along, this is an opportunity to gain insight into the shadowy realms of your mind. Conduct shadow work, not by trying to stem the flow but by being radically present and observing. Ignoring the old and attempting to stifle it will not suffice, as it will continue to rear its head. Deprogramming can only occur when you have a new belief to replace the old.

Cognitive understanding comes before the emotional level. Old emotional states can inhibit the application of new cognitive ideas. When an old belief comes up, tell yourself, "I no longer resonate with this. At my core, I believe …" and consciously think of the new idea.

Apply the knowledge each time the emotional belief arises. The conceptual change comes in time. Use your thoughts as a powerful alchemic tool; both the positive and negative will assist you in transformational healing, collapsing the old and making way for the new.

TORNGARSUK

Prioritise sleep hygiene and rest to generate energy stores, emotional peace and a focused mind. Respite will lead to the answers you seek.

Torngarsuk is the chief god within the Inuit pantheon, honoured as the god of the sky. Leader of the Tornat—a group of protective gods—Torngarsuk is thought to be immortal. His one weakness is that he can be killed by thunder. Along with being a god, he is also believed to be a demon spirit, sometimes being depicted as a one-armed warrior or a tiny man, depending on different versions of his mythology. A master of whales and seals, Torngarsuk is often called upon by fishermen for protection. Sometimes, he appeared as a bear, associated with the restorative healing found through hibernation. This is why *angakkuq*—Inuit medicine men—invoke him to assist them with those who are unwell and in need of renewed wellbeing.

TORNGARSUK'S MESSAGE

The world appears bleak, and problems are too much to bear when dealing with burnout, extreme tiredness and sensory overload. Drift away into a deep sea of tranquillity and find yourself waking up ready to face a new day with a refreshed sense of vitality and vigour.

Action and goal setting are integral elements of a well-rounded life. They help to avoid atrophy and stagnation. Conversely, relaxation and enjoying life are of equal importance. Modern society has perpetuated the notion of striving for extreme productivity and success to avoid 'laziness'. A hustle mentality has led to tiredness becoming a bragging right.

It is time to release thought patterns that hinder your happiness and wellbeing, and strive for balance. Resting does not make you lazy. You do not have to do anything to be worthy of relaxation. You are already everything you need to be.

Sleep rejuvenates you mentally, spiritually, energetically, physically and emotionally. Much is happening as you slumber. You heal in many ways during your sleeping hours, readying you for new phases. Downloads, activations and intuitive insights are received as you tap into dimensions reachable through sleep. Your subconscious works things out via your dreams.

Construct a sleep sanctuary with the temperature, cleansed energy and tools most conducive to elevated sleep quality. White noise, guided meditations and lavender oil can get you started on your sleep hygiene journey. Form morning and night routines that leave you feeling your best.

Rest can come passively through sleep and actively through restorative practices such as meditation, stretching, connecting with nature and massage. Find respite in different types of rest that rejuvenate various elements of you. Physical, mental, social, sensory, spiritual, emotional and creative rest are all required for you at different times. Incorporating abundant rest will give you renewed energy, concentration, mental clarity and productivity.

The calmative effects on your nervous system and mind will ease tension and anxious thoughts that inhibit the faculties required to think clearly and regulate your emotions. Indulge in slumber and replenishing practices and discover that everything will feel easier to tackle in the morning.

YARILO

It is prudent to have a heart that is open yet discerning. Deep connection requires openness and knowing where to place your love.

In Slavic folklore, Yarilo is simultaneously the god of war and the god of springtime. Yarilo, the tenth son of the god of thunder Perun, is recognised as a vibrant lifeforce embodying a strong polarity due to his connections with war and renewal. A life and death god, Yarilo goes through the cycle of life every year, dying in winter and bringing back spring from the Underworld when he returns to life. Yarilo caught the attention of Morana, the goddess of death and nature. They fell deeply in love and married, celebrated as the summer solstice. However, Yarilo was unfaithful to her. Morana felt so blindsided and mortified upon finding out that she killed him in a ritual (harvest time) before closing down her heart, thus turning into the hag of winter.

YARILO'S MESSAGE

In matters of the heart, it is easy to become swept away toward one extreme or the other. One severity is walking around with rose-tinted glasses, your heart on your sleeve; the other is closing the heart down in complete mistrust. There's a sweet spot bang in the middle where you can be open and perceptive simultaneously. Just as spring breaks up summer and winter, nuance is needed when falling in love to prevent the extremes from taking over.

With only openness, issues arise where love can be blind, leading to obvious breaches of trust that get ignored. Being in love with love is wonderful; however, don't let it blind you to reality. Red flags are not so visible through rose-tinted glasses. The hormones that love brings—oxytocin and norepinephrine—can lead to ignoring clear signs that someone is incompatible with you. The highs and lows of a toxic relationship can be addictive with the hits of dopamine it provides.

Soul remembrance and desire 'at first sight' are real, yet it takes time to get to know the complexity of a person and learn if you are genuinely well-matched. Chemistry doesn't always come with compatibility. Sometimes, love is not enough when you are fundamentally incompatible.

On the other hand, not ever letting anyone in and remaining shut down is equally as extreme as having no barriers to contain your love. Too many barriers block love. Not enough allows any riff-raff in. Letting someone in and then getting burned can lead you to feel like you made a mistake by trusting. This perspective puts all the power in their hands.

Another perspective is that you took a chance on love because you deserve the connection and companionship of the experience. You didn't take a chance on them. You took a chance on YOU because life is too short to play it safe all of the time. Having an open heart to the possibility of love, yet a mind that remains shrewd, is a formidable combination to behold.

Go into dating with an open mind and heart and allow things to unfold naturally, not as all or nothing. Bring your past with you as a discernment tool rather than mistrust, and see your love life bloom on a solid foundation rather than shakily built on disillusionment.

YESHUA

The stab of betrayal cuts deep, making you lose faith. Soothe your aching heart as you move through the tears and pain.

The life story of Yeshua—also known as Jesus Christ, the Lamb of God and many other titles—is perhaps one of the most widely discussed and theorised of all time. There are many narratives, religions and belief structures across the world centred around him. A highly contested topic, it is impossible to know the exact story of his life. It is theorised that Yeshua was born sometime between 6 BCE and 4 BCE. Referred to in many biblical and historical texts, he is viewed in many forms — healer, teacher, saviour and part of the Holy Spirit. There is a theory among some circles that the second coming of Christ is here in the form of Christ consciousness—or unity consciousness—within the collective at large. There's a wealth of lessons to glean from Yeshua's life and experiences, including his unwavering devotion to his cause, profound teachings, compassionate wisdom and an intimate exploration of the core human experience — marked by adversity, betrayal and resistance. The culmination of Yeshua's challenges unfolded with the betrayal by one of his apostles, Judas, ultimately leading to his crucifixion.

YESHUA'S MESSAGE

Betrayal from someone you have put your deepest trust in feels like a soul-crushing stab to the heart. It can have you questioning humanity and whether you want to place your loyalty in people anymore in both platonic and romantic relationships. Betrayal can make you feel blindsided entirely and your trust shattered into pieces. You can be left so crippled by the pain that your life comes to a temporary standstill.

Provide yourself time and space to soothe your heart, to grieve and release all the hurt. You are valid in feeling torn up; this is a time to be gentle on yourself as you mend. Allow yourself the space and time to fall apart and put the proper support systems in place to help you move through it. Using logic and distractions will draw out the process and may result in lingering resentment and difficulty in moving forward, and could be a point of contention in terms of trusting in future connections.

Sensitivity and trust are qualities to be proud of. There is no need to feel ashamed of being open and loving and for feeling deeply. Once you have given yourself space to cry, release your anger, and feel everything you need to feel; it is time for reflection.

Look back and see if any signs were indicating to you to have stronger boundaries. Sometimes, we are blindsided. Other times, we can find ourselves letting small discretions slip out of understanding and not wanting to lose connection. If, during your reflections, you feel that there were signs that were ignored, think about how you will handle similar situations in the future.

You are not to blame for bad behaviour directed at you, although it is important to hold yourself accountable for the choices you will make afterwards. Remaining open is beneficial if you desire to experience intimacy and connection, and so is honouring yourself and choosing where to place your loyalty, so you don't feel the burn of betrayal again and again. A phase will come after you process the immediate stabbing of betrayal that brings with it forgiveness, compassion, acceptance and understanding. Before this time comes, ensure that you envelop yourself with the healing needed for you, before delving into the next stage of the process. It will come in due time.

YUM KAAX

Your mind, body and spirit would benefit from a cleansing, grounding and protection process. Implement a regimen to provide clarity and an environment conducive to thriving.

In the Maya pantheon, Yum Kaax is the son of two of the most influential deities, Ixchel and Itzamná. Emulating his parents, he came to be the god of nature. The guardian of the jungle, he oversees wild vegetation and wild animals. He later became honoured by farmers as a god of agriculture, protecting crops from the wild animals and jungle. One of his principal roles was staving off drought and hunger by protecting the crops. This was done with the help of the rain god, Chaac, one of his greatest allies. Chaac would provide cleansing and nourishment through the rain, while Yum Kaax protected the crops, the earth and the hunters. Yum Kaax, translating to 'lord of the forests', oversees the protection of farmers and hunters who call on him, singing songs that will bring the hunters success and return their arrows to them. Seen as the personification of maize, he is associated with the symbol of an ear of corn.

YUM KAAX'S MESSAGE

Being a sensitive individual in a harsh world can take its toll. Your sensitivity is a beautiful gift, although it sometimes feels like a curse. Cleansing, grounding and protecting are the trifecta to build a solid energetic foundation. Challenges thrown your way are easier to withstand with a clear mind and grounded energy. Decisions become easier, emotional regulation simpler, and solutions to problems emerge quicker.

Cleansing shifts energetic debris clinging to you, some from within, some absorbed from others. Use spiritual tools such as sound bowls, black tourmaline, ethically sourced sage and essential oils. Visualise your energy field cleansing when you shower, allowing the elemental power of water to release all that no longer serves you. Implement somatic shaking — moving to an upbeat song with your feet flat on the floor. This clears your energy field and grounds you.

Grounding helps you root into the earthly experience. With an adequately anchored base chakra, you become a sturdy energy conduit, strengthening your intuition. Get amongst nature and connect with the ground barefoot to feel centred and calm.

The earth is a conductor; its negatively charged ions neutralise positively charged ions within you upon contact, benefitting your health. A tree with weak roots gets blown away in the slightest wind, and a deeply rooted oak tree can withstand the pressure of an extreme gale. Stand firm in the eye of the storm.

Protecting your energy makes staying clear, centred and grounded maintainable for longer. Utilise obsidian, frankincense oil, runes and protective mist sprays; listen to solfeggio-frequency music; visualise a protective bubble around you during meditation.

Affirming your boundaries, saying "no" when you want to, and remaining mindful of who you spend your time around are massive contributors to protection. Recognise when you need to love someone from afar instead of continuing to absorb their energetics.

Taking as little as five minutes in the morning and five at night to cleanse, ground and protect your energy can make a significant difference to the elevation of your state, including emotional regulation and stability, easier decision making, feeling centred and calm and a clear mind.

ABOUT THE AUTHOR

Christabel Jessica, originally from the traditional lands of the Gubbi Gubbi Nation in Queensland, Australia, began her exploration of the human experience at the young age of two. Even then, she wandered, asking, "How are you feeling?" — a question that has become the hallmark of her empathetic and intuitive nature.

Christabel's early path led her to study Early Childhood Education, a journey she later redirected toward Psychology. Yet, her insatiable desire for spiritual exploration led her to an unexpected turn. Two days after attending a reiki workshop, she bravely chose to chart a new course, delving into psychic development and intuitive healing. With an unquenchable thirst for knowledge, she consumed spiritual wisdom as if it were her university curriculum.

Though the twists and turns of her educational journey might seem perplexing, Christabel now recognises the profound purpose behind each choice. Her exploration of education and the human mind, both scientifically and spiritually, uniquely equips her to offer a transformative blend of insights. Through YouTube videos, oracle decks and healing sessions, Christabel shares her wisdom, guiding those who, like her, feel compelled to dismantle old paradigms in favour of the new.

Christabel extends her passion into creating a nurturing haven for spiritual seekers, providing a safe space for healing and growth.

As the creator of the *Goddess Within Oracle*, her contributions to the spiritual realm resonate with wisdom, sensitivity and authenticity.

Embark on your spiritual journey with Christabel Jessica at **www.christabeljessica.com** where she invites you to explore, learn and transform.

ABOUT THE ARTIST

A self-taught illustrator with a degree in art history, Cecilia G.F. uses her knowledge of symbology and art theory to enrich her works with meaning. She draws inspiration from many sources, including music, books, video games and mythology.

Cecilia has collaborated with publishers such as Alethé, Supersonic, Nocturna, Kakao Books and Munyx and worked with clients from all over the world. Some of her best-known cover images are Clorofilia by Cristina Jurado (for which she won the Ignotus Award in 2018), La Compañía Amable by Rocío Vega, Sistemas Críticos by Martha Wells and El Clan Sin Nombre by África Vázquez Beltrán.

Discover more of Cecilia's works by connecting with ThanatosofNicte on Twitter, Instagram and Twitch, or Ceciliagf on ArtStation.

More from Blue Angel Publishing®

Goddess Within Oracle

HEALING WITH THE DIVINE FEMININE

Christabel Jessica

Artwork by Cecilia G.F. & Dannielle Jones

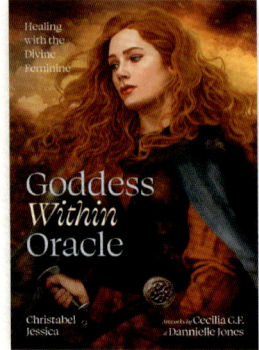

Your Wise Woman Awakens. A barefoot maiden whispers of magic beneath the slender moon, a wizened crone prepares healing herbs in a woodland cottage, and elsewhere across time and place, an anointed priestess lights a candle to begin her temple ritual. The energy of the Goddess is with them all. Place your feet firmly on the earth, breathe into your bold and gracious heart, and feel her rise within you.

ISBN: 978-1-922573-79-7
44 cards & 160-page full-colour guidebook.

More from Blue Angel Publishing®

The Alchemist's Oracle

ELIXIRS FOR PERSONAL GROWTH & WELLBEING

Zoe Sadler

Set out on an enchanting journey with *The Alchemist's Oracle*, where ancient alchemy brews a magical concoction of self-transformation. Step into the mystical realms where ordinary life merges with the extraordinary, revealing secrets to illuminate your path. Within this bewitching deck, each card is a potion, an elixir for your soul. Unlock the wisdom of the alchemical symbols and elements, guiding you through a playful odyssey of self-discovery.

ISBN: 978-1-922574-25-1
48 cards & 176-page full-colour guidebook. Features gold-foil stamping on front cover.

More from Blue Angel Publishing®

Dracones Loqui

Ravynne Phelan

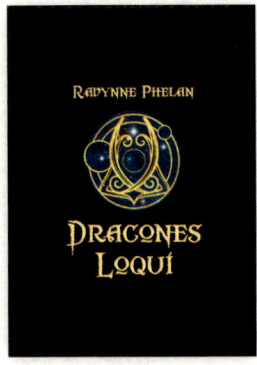

Welcome, seeker, to *Dracones Loqui* **('Dragons Speak')** — A realm where dreams take flight, realities intertwine, and whispers of the Divine echo through the corridors of eternity.

You are welcomed to this sacred space of connection to the mystical and reverence for dragon wisdom. Each card you draw is a portal to timeless, boundless love and celestial guidance. May the dragons' presence empower you on your quest for healing and self-discovery, leading you closer to the magic within.

ISBN: 978-1-922574-26-8
54 circular cards & 160-page full-colour guidebook.
Gold-foil stamping on box, card backs, and gold-painted card edges.

More from Blue Angel Publishing®

The Secret Language of Darkness

SOUL LIGHT TRANSMISSIONS FROM THE SHADOW

Denise Jarvie

Artwork by Daniel B. Holeman

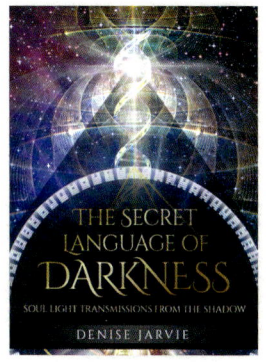

Unlock the secrets of your inner world with *The Secret Language of Darkness.* An inner repository of all the sensations and experiences you've disowned, your shadow is part of you, and it longs to be embraced and belong. Discover the hidden messages and beliefs that hold you back from your best life. Through shadow mastery classes and insightful card messages, you'll gain the skills to face and integrate repressed aspects of your personality.

ISBN: 978-1-922574-16-9
45 cards & 216-page full-colour guidebook. Features gold-foil stamping on front cover.

For more information on this or
any Blue Angel Publishing release,
please visit our website at:

WWW.BLUEANGELONLINE.COM